MESSENGERS FROM THE DEAD

MESSENGERS FROM THE DEAD

Literature of the Holocaust

by IRVING HALPERIN

THE WESTMINSTER PRESS · Philadelphia

ISBN 0-664-20892-4

LIBRARY OF CONGRESS CATALOG CARD NO. 77–118623

Grateful acknowledgment is made to the following for permission to use quotations from their publications:

Beacon Press, *Man's Search for Meaning,* by Viktor E. Frankl. Copyright © 1959, 1962 by Viktor Frankl. Used by permission of Hodder & Stoughton Ltd.

B'nai B'rith, Commission on Adult Jewish Education, "On Being a Jew," by Elie Wiesel, *Jewish Heritage,* Summer 1967; "On the Writing and Reading of Holocaust Literature," by Irving Halperin, *Jewish Heritage,* Spring 1968.

Commentary, "Eichmann's Victims and the Unheard Testimony," by Elie Wiesel. Copyright © 1961 by the American Jewish Committee.

Hill & Wang, Inc., *Night,* by Elie Wiesel, tr. by Stella Rodway. English translation © MacGibbon & Kee, 1960.

Holt, Rinehart and Winston, Inc., *The Gates of the Forest,* by Elie Wiesel, tr. by Frances Frenaye. Copyright © 1966 by Holt, Rinehart and Winston, Inc.

The Macmillan Company, *Scroll of Agony: The Warsaw Diary of Chaim A. Kaplan,* tr. and ed. by Abraham I. Katsh. Copyright © by Abraham I. Katsh, 1965.

The Orion Press, *If This Is a Man,* by Primo Levi.

The Vanguard Press, Inc., *Night of the Mist,* by Eugene Heimler. © Eugene Heimler, 1959.

PUBLISHED BY THE WESTMINSTER PRESS ®
PHILADELPHIA, PENNSYLVANIA

PRINTED IN THE UNITED STATES OF AMERICA

FOR MY WIFE

Contents

Contents

Acknowledgments

Parts of this book have appeared in different form in *Conservative Judaism, Hadassah Magazine, Jewish Book Annual,* 1968, 1969 (Jewish Book Council of America, National Jewish Welfare Board), *Jewish Heritage, Jewish Life, Judaism, The Nation, Yad Vashem Studies* (VII), and in *The Jewish Catastrophe in Europe,* edited by Judah Pilch (The American Association for Jewish Education, 1968).

I have been aided by a generous grant from the National Foundation for Jewish Culture and Hadassah. Thanks are also due to San Francisco State College for a faculty research leave.

I wish to thank Arthur A. Cohen, who originally suggested that I write a book on Holocaust literature. Part of the research for this study was done at the Yad Vashem Archives in Jerusalem, and there Dr. Livia Rothkirchen put her vast knowledge of the Holocaust freely at my disposal. Among many others to whom I feel special gratitude for various kinds of help are Zdena Berger (whose profoundly moving first novel, *Tell Me Another Morning,* gave this book its first impetus), Rabbi Bernard Ducoff, Samuel Halperin, Dr. Judah Pilch, Rabbi Harold Schulweis, Rabbi Saul White, Elie Wiesel, and Herbert Wilner. Above and beyond all other help, I have had the active assistance and patient forbearance of my wife, Tam H. Halperin.

I. H.

San Francisco, California

I

On the Writing and Reading
of Holocaust Literature

Why are so many in the audience weeping? For the man speaking to them, for his suffering? There are lawyers and doctors in the audience, and I had presumed that members of these professions are not easily given to weeping in public. What chords has the speaker struck to make them sit with lowered heads, staring fixedly at the floor?

And why, instead of looking at the faces of the audience, are the eyes of the speaker directed toward the top of the hall's rear wall—and perhaps far beyond? To whom is he addressing his remarks? To an image of the dead, to those millions who did not survive?

"In deference to your large suffering," Alyosha Karamazov says, falling on his knees before his brother Ivan. Similarly, in the presence of Elie Wiesel, the speaker, one feels Alyosha's impulse. It is impossible to describe the marks of suffering on this man's face; the expression in his eyes is of one who has come out of hell. Not without reason did the French writer François Mauriac look into those eyes and weep; ". . . that look, as of a Lazarus risen from the dead, yet still a prisoner within the grim confines where he has strayed, stumbling among the shameful corpses." What especially distressed Mauriac during his meeting with Wiesel is that the latter, who as a boy in Hungary had been a devotedly observant Jew, no longer had religious faith; for him God had died in Auschwitz. And yet this Lazarus seemed to Mauriac, himself a believer, far from broken but, on the contrary, strong—strong in that he was the accuser; he accused God of having abandoned one third of European Jewry. Mauriac had the urge to speak to the young Wiesel about Christ and the cross, the mystery and grace of human sacrifice and resurrection. But instead, looking at the "angelic sadness" of the other's eyes, the older man "could only embrace him, weeping."

Is that why many in the audience are weeping? Do they hear in the speaker's voice and see on his face what Mauriac experienced?

Much of what happened during the Holocaust resides in the realm of the incomprehensible. Some have said that there can be no explanation for the destruction of European Jewry; hence Alfred Kazin's reported response to the question of whether he thought there was any meaning behind the slaughter of the 6,000,000—"I hope not." [1] So, too, Wiesel, who was directly marked by the tragedy, still does not "understand." In reviewing Bernd Naumann's *Auschwitz* on the Frankfurt trial, he writes:

> The trial taught us nothing new about the holocaust, which still transcends all dimensions of consciousness. We still cannot grasp how it all happened and why. The mystery remains intact. And just as we will never be able to penetrate the harrowing memory of the victim, so we cannot peer into the twisted mind of the assassin. Everything to do with Auschwitz must, in the end, lead into darkness. [2]

And at a recent symposium he said: "The Holocaust defies parallels. Did it really happen? Maybe not. I often wonder." [3]

Perhaps we shall never understand what the Holocaust was, yet this limitation does not free us of the moral responsibility to keep asking questions of it. [4] And because they are unanswerable questions, they are none the less significant. Certain questions are put to mankind, Tolstoy said, not that man should answer them, but that he should go on trying.

It is not the desire to effect instant catharsis that impels survivors like Wiesel to write and speak out. They hardly want
their books or public statements to be used for a cheap emotional lift. In their eyes, those who use the Holocaust in this way
have not yet *felt* the tragedy; it has not yet turned to blood and
ashes within them. Had that inner transformation occurred,
they would be moved not merely to tears but to hate and anger
as well—hate for what took place during the Hitler years. A
"justified" [5] hate, as Elie Wiesel has remarked, of those who
forced children to look at the hideous face of absolute evil.
Anger because the world, Jews[6] and non-Jews alike, was mainly
silent when the victims were being destroyed. Anger like
the kind of wounded outrage that informs Picasso's painting
Guernica. Or the kind of hate and anger powerfully rendered
by Schwarz-Bart in *The Last of the Just*: the incident, for example, when Ernie Levy, having been assaulted and humiliated
by Hitler Youth hooligans, in turn destroys scores of insects in
a meadow.

If not as catalysts of "instant catharsis," how, then, are
survivor-writers like Elie Wiesel to be viewed? Essentially as
moral teachers. "Messengers from the dead," [7] wanting to bear
witness,[8] they bring us reports (i.e., eyewitness accounts, diaries,
poems, short stories, novels, plays); reports written with a sense
of urgency, as though the writers sought to justify both their
own survival and what they have written against the dark background of the Holocaust. Hence Eugene Heimler, author of
Night of the Mist, after being liberated from a concentration
camp, resolved:

> There were . . . messages I had to deliver to the living
> from the dead. There were things I had to do, words I had
> to speak, moments which I had to dissect in order to show
> the world what I had seen and lived through, on behalf
> of the millions who had seen it also—but could no longer
> speak. Of their dead, burnt, bodies I would be the voice.[9]

What is the central intention behind these "messages"? Mainly
it is to teach the reader by interrogating him. The messengers,

in effect, ask the reader to rigorously examine his knowledge
of and relationship to the Holocaust, and they do so by posing
difficult questions. Such as? How was it possible for some prisoners to remain remarkably human despite the brutalizing conditions of the camps? How was it possible for prisoners to
exercise what Dr. Viktor Frankl refers to as "the last of human
freedoms"—the ability to "choose one's attitude in any given set
of circumstances"? How should one assess Primo Levi's con-
tention in *If This Is a Man* that *only* by sacrificing personal
dignity and honor could one evade annihilation by the Nazis?

These difficult and painful questions are not addressed to
those who complain: "Enough! Too depressing. Let's discuss
more cheerful subjects. Besides, we've already heard too much
on the subject. Now we need to try and forget all that." (Sometimes their sentiments evoke those voices in contemporary
Germany which clamor for an immediate end to the war crimes
trials.) Their attitude therein evokes the words of the Israeli
poet, Yehuda Amihai—"Most people in our time have the face
of Lot's wife, turned toward the Holocaust and yet always
escaping."

Neither are these questions addressed to those who are
ashamed to speak to their children and to young people about
the destruction of European Jewry. It is as though they have
accepted, uncritically, the myth that the Jews of Europe went
to their death as sheep to slaughter. They tend to shy away from
discussing the Holocaust, as though the subject shamed them—
how bitterly ironic that Jews should assume a burden of shame
because *their* own people were murdered!—and hence was
something to be put out of sight.

But why need the story of the Jewish catastrophe produce
such shame? If one can be proud of the Zealots at Masada and
the martyrdom of Jews at the Inquisition stakes, no Jew need
hang his head in discussing the recent European tragedy. Wiesel
is eloquent on this point:

> Why then do we admittedly think of the Holocaust with
> shame? Why don't we claim it as a glorious chapter of our

eternal history? After all, it did change man and his world
—well, it did not change man, but it did change the world.
It is still the greatest event in our times. Why then are we
ashamed of it? In its power it even influenced language.
Negro quarters are called ghettos; Hiroshima is explained
by Auschwitz; Vietnam is described in terms which were
used one generation ago. Everything today revolves around
our Holocaust experience. Why then do we face it with
such ambiguity? Perhaps this should be the task of Jewish
educators and philosophers; to reopen the event as a source
of pride, to take it back into our history. Who knows? The
dead did not really die; their tale is ours. Perhaps they
sing, and we are unable to hear. We are afraid of their
song, of their pride.[10]

In any event, the story of the Holocaust cannot be readily
swept under a rug; neither can its enormity and significance be
de-emphasized. If not a measure of twentieth-century man, it
at the least was, as Elie Wiesel has stated, one of the two most
important events in Jewish history, the other being Sinai. And
because Jewish history is turned toward Sinai and Auschwitz,
the Jew has, Wiesel contends, a unique obligation:

> Any Jew born before, during, or after the Holocaust must
> *enter it again in order to take it upon himself.* [Italics mine.]
> We all stood at Sinai, we all shared the same vision there;
> we all heard the *Anochi*—"I am the Lord. . . ." If this
> is true, then we are also linked to Auschwitz.[11]

And as the covenant came out of Mt. Sinai, so too has a new
Bible, a new kind of literature, emerged from the Holocaust.
Describing the stories prisoners in Auschwitz would tell one
another, stories of the lives they had left behind them and tales
of their ordeals in the camps, Primo Levi writes in *If This Is a
Man*: "We tell them to each other in the evening, and they take
place in Norway, Italy, Algeria, the Ukraine, and are simple
and incomprehensible like the stories in the Bible. But are they
not themselves stories of a new Bible?"

They certainly are often painful stories. But this condition does not entitle us to back away from attempting to comprehend them. As Hannah Arendt maintains in *The Origins of Totalitarianism*: "Comprehension does not mean denying the outrageous. . . . It means examining and bearing consciously the burden which our century has placed on us—neither denying its existence nor submitting meekly to its weight."

These documents and imaginative works have been submitted to us so that we may "face up to" the kind of hell men created in the twentieth century. They forcefully remind us that if a particular society was so murderous, we ought to be doubly alert to the murderous instincts, the Hitler-Himmler-Eichmann impulses in our own nature. Primo Levi understands this: "If from inside the Lager, a message could have seeped out to free men, it would have been this: take care not to suffer in your own homes what is inflicted on us here."

Not that the messages of these documents and stories are generally positive or instructive in tone and content. Some imply that, given the unspeakable desecration of human life during the Holocaust, perhaps it would have been better for many of the persecuted to have died rather than survive. The testimony of a witness at the Frankfurt trial of the Auschwitz guards supports this view:

> I once walked through a barrack filled with corpses, all of them stripped. Then I saw something moving between the corpses, and that something wasn't nude. It was a young girl. I pulled her to the outside and said: "Who are you?" She said she was a Greek Jewess from Salonika. "How long have you been here?" "I don't know." "Why are you here?" And she answered: "I can no longer live with the ones alive. I prefer to be with the dead." I gave her a piece of bread. By nightfall she was dead.[12]

"I prefer to be with the dead." This line needs to be repeated again and again, for it points to the darkest reaches of the European tragedy. The thoughts of a man living in hell would move from anger and disgust to complete despair. If finally he preferred to die rather than to survive, it often was because he believed that in such an inferno no just man would want to continue living. In this connection, Elie Wiesel cites the story of a victim who might have survived but preferred to be with the dead.

> There comes to mind . . . the case of the woman who, naked and wounded, had managed to escape from the ditch, the mass grave in which all the Jews of her town were mowed down by German machine guns. That woman returned to the ditch after a little while to rejoin the phantasmagoric community of corpses. Miraculously saved, she still could not accept a life which in her eyes had become impure.[13]

Perhaps this account suggests why many survivors hold themselves in contempt for having survived. For them the obsessive question is—"Why are *you alive* when the others are not?" Elie Wiesel has written on the burden of such survivors:

> Their tragedy is the tragedy of Job before his submission; they believe themselves to be guilty, though they are not. Only a Great Judge would have it in his power to rid them of this burden. But in their eyes no one possesses either such authority or such power: no one, either human or divine.
>
> Therefore they prefer, in this condemned world, not to hurl their defiance at men and their anger into the face of history, but to keep silent, to pursue the monologue which only the dead deserve to hear.[14]

Dark chords, then, in a literature of fire and ashes. Yet there are those reports which allow for at least a semblance of hope. Some writers stand in awe of the survivors, as though their very physical presence testifies to the mystery and miracle of survival itself. They suggest that man will continue to survive because he has a spirit capable of extraordinary resilience and endurance. Other writers pay homage to the many instances of spiritual resistance exercised by Jews in the camps and ghettos. Still others articulate the belief that men have a chance to protest against human suffering by alleviating it in others.

But whatever the nature of these reports, whether they speak in apocalyptic accents on the death of man and God or whether they bear witness to the mystery of survival and man's capacity for endurance and compassion, what gives them commonality is their urgent sense of purpose. They are written by those who wish, as George Steiner has remarked, "to discover the relations between those done to death and those alive then, and the relations of both to us; to locate, as exactly as record and imagination are able, the measure of unknowing, indifference, complicity, commission which relates the contemporary or survivor to the slain." [15] Similarly, in a symposium, "Jewish Values in the Post-Holocaust Future," which took place on March 26, 1967 (see Summer 1967 issue of *Judaism*), Steiner, one of the participants, responded to the question, "Why should we tell the story of the Holocaust?" posed by a fellow participant, Elie Wiesel:

> To answer your question, Elie, why should we try and tell about the Holocaust experience at all? . . . We must tell it to be on our guard, so that our children know when it may happen the next time. You know better than I, Elie, that in France there were two modes of horror when one was in the trains. One was to be with your child and to know why you were going—because you are a Jew. Worse, was to have to explain to your children, as countless assimilationists did: *"Qu'est-ce que c'est qu'un juif? Pourquoi moi?"*—Why I? What is all this about? Thus we owe to our children . . . to say: Be on your guard! Know the signals! If it be Argentina tomorrow, or Morocco two years from now, or South Africa when the hell may break loose— and this is coming as certain as we sit here—it is your and my task to save whom we can. I think it is worth telling the story, so we can tell the noise when it comes and be on our toes, and know how to move.

The writer (and by extension, the reader) of Holocaust literature is asked to remember and to speak out. There is a Biblical injunction that addresses itself directly to this historic responsibility:

Tell ye your children of it,
And let your children tell their children,
And their children another generation.
(Joel 1:3.)

This injunction Elie Wiesel clearly recognizes and accepts. He believes that his moral obligation as a writer is to keep speaking out on the horrors and madness of the recent past, lest the road that led from Auschwitz to Hiroshima could lead to a nuclear holocaust. At least this would seem to be the message of one of his favorite fables, recorded by the French newspaper *L'Express,* June 6, 1963:

There was once a very wise king who was warned strangely in a dream: the next harvest in his land would be cursed and whoever would eat of it would go mad. The king then called his most faithful counsellor and said, "I will put provisions into your house so that you will be able to avoid the common fate. Thus, when we are all mad, you can go through the kingdom and in all the streets of the cities, in the fields before the cottages, you will cry constantly, 'My brothers, remember that you are mad.' " (P. 34.)

After the gates of the concentration camps were flung open by the Allied troops in 1945, survivors began to write about their experiences. Twenty-five years later they are still writing. There is an immense body of material on the victims and the survivors. Some have paid homage to the piety of the martyrs who went to their deaths in the spirit of *kiddush ha-shem.* Others, like Bruno Bettelheim, have written of the death instinct in the victims, of how, supposedly, this instinct paralyzed them, so that they were unable to fight back against the Nazis. Hannah Arendt, for example, has spoken of the "banality of evil" in Nazi officials like Eichmann. Still others have been concerned to show how some of the ghettos did fight back even as the enemy stood at their gates.

But whatever the content or approach, whether through scholarly investigation or fiction, most of the writers contributing to Holocaust literature have sought to elucidate the issues and implications relevant to an understanding of the Holocaust. They do not deny that much of what happened during the catastrophe is incomprehensible; nonetheless, through their writing they are attempting to attain a measure of clarification.

This study is generated by a similar intent. I, who was not there, feel linked to Auschwitz and am trying, in the words of Wiesel, to "discover it now." I wish to "understand" a semblance of the incomprehensible. To exercise this intent, I will examine a number of representative works, fiction and nonfiction, in English, that deal with various aspects of the Holocaust.

The following chapters will consider some representative works of Holocaust literature in English, selected from three genres: the eyewitness accounts, as they are referred to, or personal narratives; diaries; and fiction. Why these three genres to the exclusion of others? Very simply, because the best writing in translation I know of has appeared in these three forms rather than in, say, drama or poetry. There are, of course, some important Holocaust poems and plays such as the poems of Nelly Sachs, Jacob Glatstein, Yitzhak Katznelson, and the plays *The Deputy, The Investigation, The Condemned of Altona*. But a few stars do not a constellation make; and, in any event, not many poems and plays can stand alongside of *Last of the Just, Night, The Town Beyond the Wall, The Gates of the Forest, If This Is a Man, From Death-Camp to Existentialism,* Ringelblum's *Notes from the Warsaw Ghetto,* and Kaplan's *Scroll of Agony.*

As to the chronology of this study, I shall begin with the eyewitness accounts, move on to Kaplan's Warsaw ghetto diary, proceed to an examination of Wiesel's five novels, and conclude with a look at some works of fiction stressing the theme of spiritual resistance. Why this particular arrangement? Because it seems sensible to take up at the outset those works which are highly explicit and uncomplicated in form; and, conversely, to leave for the latter part of the study the fiction, which is more subtly organized. Again, the personal narratives and diaries speak directly and openly to the reader; their various presentations and effects do not depend upon obliqueness, indirection, halftone, and nuance, as is generally the case in the fiction.

There is, for example, no easy passage for the reader through the labyrinths and networks of parables, midrashic and talmudic sayings, rabbinical legends, aphorisms, and cabbalistic fantasies in Wiesel's five novels. At the least, the reader coming to these books ought to anticipate a struggle; the possession of their content calls for Jacob-like wrestling. Ultimately, it is not the reader who reads them but they who "read" the reader; they interrogate and challenge his *raison d'être,* the very foundations of his existence.

All the examined works in this study have a common denominator: they are unmistakably informed by a sense of mission; they offer to "bear witness." And the authors of these works have attempted, in the previously quoted words of Elie Wiesel, to "enter it [the Holocaust] again in order to take" its dark legacy upon themselves.

2

Meaning and Despair
in the Literature of the Survivors

We stumbled on in the darkness, over big stones and through large puddles, along the one road leading from the camp. The accompanying guards kept shouting at us and driving us with the butts of their rifles. Anyone with very sore feet supported himself on his neighbor's arm. Hardly a word was spoken; the icy wind did not encourage talk. Hiding his mouth behind his upturned collar, the man marching next to me whispered suddenly: "If our wives could see us now! I do hope they are better off in their camps and don't know what is happening to us."

That brought thoughts of my own wife to mind. And as we stumbled on for miles, slipping on icy spots, supporting each other time and again, dragging one another up and onward, nothing was said, but we both knew: each of us was thinking of his wife. Occasionally I looked at the sky, where the stars were fading and the pink light of the morning was beginning to spread behind a dark bank of clouds. But my mind clung to my wife's image, imagining it with uncanny acuteness. I heard her answering me, saw her smile, her frank and encouraging look. Real or not, her look was then more luminous than the sun which was beginning to rise.

—Viktor Frankl, *From Death-Camp to Existentialism*

So our nights drag on. The dream of Tantalus and the dream of the story are woven into a texture of more in-

distinct images: the suffering of the day, composed of hunger, blows, cold, exhaustion, fear and promiscuity, turns
at night-time into shapeless nightmares of unheard-of
violence, which in free life would only occur during a fever.
One wakes up at every moment, frozen with terror, shaking
in every limb, under the impression of an order shouted
out by a voice full of anger in a language not understood.
The procession to the bucket and the thud of bare heels
on the wooden floor turns into another symbolic procession: it is us again, grey and identical, small as ants, yet
so huge as to reach up to the stars, bound one against the
other, countless, covering the plain as far as the horizon;
sometimes melting into a single substance, a sorrowful
turmoil in which we all feel ourselves trapped and suffo-
cated; sometimes marching in a circle, without beginning or
end, with a blinding giddiness and a sea of nausea rising
from the praecordia to the gullet; until hunger or cold or
the fullness of our bladders turn our dreams into their
customary forms.

                              —Primo Levi, *If This Is a Man*

   Felled to the ground, stunned with blows, the old man
cried:
   "Meir. Meir, my boy! Don't you recognize me? I'm
your father . . . you're hurting me . . . you're killing
your father! I've got some bread . . . for you too . . .
for you too . . ."
   He collapsed. His fist was still clenched around a small
piece. He tried to carry it to his month. But the other one
threw himself upon him and snatched it. The old man
again whispered something, let out a rattle, and died amid
the general indifference. His son searched him, took the
bread, and began to devour it. He was not able to get
very far. Two men had seen and hurled themselves upon
him. Others joined in. When they withdrew, next to me
were two corpses, side by side, the father and the son.
   I was fifteen years old.

                                 —Elie Wiesel, *Night*

I learnt that within me, as in others, the murderer and the humanitarian exist side by side; the weak child with the voracious male. That I am not in any way superior, that I am not different from others, that I am but a link in the great chain, was among the greatest discoveries of my life. From then on I resolved to support those who fell, even as I had been supported. When someone was despicable, greedy and selfish, I remembered all the occasions when I, too, had been despicable, greedy and selfish. Buchenwald taught me to be tolerant of myself, and by that means tolerant to others.

It may be that I would have learnt this without the lesson of Buchenwald. But I would have learnt it much later—perhaps too late.

—Eugene Heimler, *Night of the Mist*

Four statements by four authors and two essential points of view: to survive as a prisoner in the camps one had to descend to the level of animals; and, conversely, despite the brutalizing conditions in the camps, it was possible for a prisoner to be impressively human. There is, of course, nothing unique about this two-sided observation. One would expect that there were as many different kinds of behavior among the prisoners as there were environmental differences from camp to camp; for example, it was generally easier for a prisoner in a so-called model camp like Sachsenhausen to maintain a semblance of composure than for prisoners who were exposed to substantially greater hardships and pressures in Auschwitz. All this is to underscore the self-evident: so many prisoners, so many conditions. Therefore it is not for us to assert cavalierly that this or that former prisoner conducted himself commendably whereas this or that prisoner carried on badly. Especially those of us who were spared the ordeal of being "there" have not earned the right to make such value judgments.

Then why the opening four quotations and the above statement about the two essential points of view they represent? For one, this arrangement is intended to provide a principle of organization for some key issues in the personal narratives. Also, the views represented by the above quotations underscore the opposing evaluations of some survivor-writers as they look back at the past: those, on the one hand, who contend that in a time when men bestially defiled and disfigured the bodies and spirits of other men, suicide or madness or nihilism for any self-respecting person would have been understandable. They aver that there was no such thing as "transcending" one's suffering in the camps, that the Nazis were beasts and they made beasts of the prisoners. And, on the other hand, those survivor-writers who believe that many of the oppressed in the camps were ennobled by their suffering.

What follows, then, is an examination of some widely acclaimed personal narratives. In this genre I include Elie Wiesel's autobiographical novel, *Night,* whose point of view and essential manner is that of personal narration.

Such an unbearably depressing body of literature. But are there any places in it that "lift up" the reader? In affirmative response to this question, we can look to *From Death-Camp to Existentialism,* by Viktor Frankl, a professor of psychiatry and neurology at the University of Vienna, who was imprisoned for three years at Auschwitz and other camps. A number of incidents in this important book point up the spiritual resources of some remarkable human beings. First, there is the unforgettable scene where Frankl buoys up the spirits of his fellow prisoners. This incident happened at a time when the morale of the men in his hut was at a dangerously low point. Hungry and cold, plagued by lice, illnesses, and severe depression, they despaired of going on; it seemed to them that their suffering was senseless, that it would be better to give up, die, and be done with the daily torture. From such despair the next step downward was to become a Mussulman, a member of the living dead, they who were almost beyond pain. In this dark moment a senior block warden, knowing of Frankl's background as a psychiatrist, persuaded him to offer his disconsolate comrades a "medical care for their souls."

One evening after work, Frankl spoke to them. He sought to

instill in them a justification, a moral sanction for attempting to live through their unbearable circumstances. He encouraged them to bear their suffering with whatever dignity was possible; to be, in short, as Dostoevsky used the phrase—and Frankl frequently alludes to it—worthy of their suffering. As the present was a nightmare, he began by speaking to them of the past and future.

Frankl himself is ailing, hungry, cold, despondent; so he is scarcely in a frame of mind to minister to others. Yet he says that their situation, though extremely grave, is not altogether futile; some of them will survive; they need to "hold on" and hope for the best. But it would not have taken an extraordinary man to say this much to them. Inmates of the camps frequently exhorted one another to hold on, to *iberlebyn*[16] (to remain alive). What makes Frankl's exhortation distinctive is the depth and power of his remarks. Even if they perish, he suggests, whatever they have experienced in the past is not lost.

> Again I quoted a poet—to avoid sounding like a preacher myself—who had written, *"Was Du erlebst, kann keine Macht der Welt Dir rauben."* (What you have experienced, no power on earth can take from you.) Not only our experiences, but all we have done . . . and all we have suffered, all this is not lost, though it is past; we have brought it into being. Having been is also a kind of being, and perhaps the surest kind. (Pp. 82–83.)

Then he returns to the present, to their situation in the camp. His comrades lie motionless, listening attentively, as he goes on to speak of the spiritual challenge before each man: the necessity to be "worthy" of one's suffering and to find some meaning in their situation.

> I told my comrades . . . that human life, under any circumstances, never ceases to have a meaning, and that this infinite meaning of life includes suffering and dying, privation and death. I asked the poor creatures who listened to me attentively in the darkness of the hut to face up to the

seriousness of our position. They must not lose hope but should keep their courage in the certainty that the hopelessness of our struggle did not detract from its dignity and meaning. I said that someone looks down on each of us in difficult hours—a friend, a wife, somebody alive or dead, or a God—and he would not expect us to disappoint him. He would hope to find us suffering proudly—not miserably —knowing how to die. (P. 83.)

"Knowing how to die . . ." [17] How remarkable! To encourage one another to die with dignity in, of all places, an extermination camp! His words invoke accounts of observant Jews who went to their deaths in the gas chambers with heads high, backs straight, singing *Ani Maamin* ("I Believe"). So, too, in *The Holocaust Kingdom,* Lena Donat recalls the way in which some Greek Jewish women went to the gas chambers (p. 306):

> When they went to their deaths they sang the "Hatikvah," the song of an old people which has always carried the vision of Zion in its heart. Since then every time I hear "Hatikvah" I always see them, the dregs of human misery, and I know that through mankind flows a stream of eternity greater and more powerful than individual deaths.

What was the immediate result of Frankl's remarks to his comrades? He remembers that at the conclusion of his words, he saw "the miserable figures of my friends limping toward me to thank me with tears in their eyes." Frankl does not consider this response an occasion for self-congratulation; for in the sentence directly following the one just cited, he adds: "But I have to confess here that only too rarely had I the inner strength to make contact with my companions in suffering and that I must have missed many opportunities for doing so."

How are we to view this incident? Men are ill, in pain; they need food, warmth. Frankl offers them only words—yet the words touch responsive chords in them, and they come forward to express their gratitude. In other parts of the camp, the SS are sadistically humiliating, torturing, murdering. Defenseless men and women are shot; Germans dispose of thousands with phenol injections; prisoners are hanged on the courtyard gallows; the infamous camp official, Boger, employs his "typewriter" [18] with zeal. These are the cultured and civilized Germans. By contrast, Frankl and his comrades, these "subhumans," probe into the farthest reaches of the spirit while the "superior" Aryans lash out with truncheons and fists. So that when Frankl's comrades come toward him with tears of gratitude in their eyes, one can grasp why there was a genuine release of spiritual elation in Auschwitz.

There are other equally moving incidents in the book. To dwell lovingly on the image of one's wife and to take immense pleasure from seeing the forms of nature, these, too, were ways of giving meaning to one's wretched existence in the camps. Such observation and reflection helped Frankl to find a *why* to live, for—to recall Nietzsche's saying: "He who has a *why* to live for can bear almost any *how*."

One "why" was through love. Although he had no way of knowing where she was—or whether she was even still alive—Frankl often thought of his wife. Nothing, he avows, could diminish the strength of his love.

> Had I known then that my wife was dead, I think that I would still have given myself, undisturbed by that knowledge, to the contemplation of her image, and that my mental conversation with her would have been just as vivid and just as satisfying. "Set me like a seal upon thy heart, love is as strong as death." (Pp. 37–38.)

In the camp, men are proficient in the means of hate, Nazi-style, and yet Frankl wills to love! He is mercilessly beaten with the butts of rifles, forced to walk for miles through darkness and over ice; and yet, astonishingly, his mind clings to an image of his wife. Sometimes the intensity and radiance of this image makes it more real than the all too palpable landmarks of fences, huts, watchtowers, crematoria. And once, in a particularly black moment, Frankl feels he has grasped the deeper meaning of human love.

A thought transfixed me: for the first time in my life I saw the truth as it is set into song by so many poets, proclaimed as the final wisdom by so many thinkers. The truth—that love is the ultimate and the highest goal to which man can aspire. Then I grasped the meaning of the greatest secret that human poetry and human thought and belief have to impart: *The salvation of man is through love and in love.* I understood how a man who has nothing left in this world still may know bliss, be it only for a brief moment, in the contemplation of his beloved. (P. 36.)

The point is that it was in Auschwitz, in *anus mundi,* as the Nazis referred to it, he perceived this truth; before then it apparently had been for him only a theoretical generalization. Thus, in the greatest extermination center of recorded history, Frankl experienced on his very pulses the validity of love as the "final wisdom."

Just as it is remarkable that his devotion transcended the physical absence of his wife, so, too, not even the coldest winter days nor the abuse of the guards could blunt his feelings for her. He would recall her face, voice, and this would help to sustain him through cycles of exhaustion, hunger, depression. On one occasion, a freezing winter dawn, as he was at work in a trench under the surveillance of a sadistic guard, he seems to have had a mystical experience.

For hours I stood hacking at the icy ground. The guard passed by, insulting me, and once again I communed with my beloved. More and more I felt that she was present, that she was with me; I had the feeling that I was able to touch her, able to stretch out my hand and grasp hers. The feeling was very strong: she was *there.* Then, at that very moment, a bird flew down silently and perched just in front of me, on the heap of soil which I had dug up from the ditch, and looked steadily at me. (P. 40.)

Still, what is one such inspiring moment, it may be asked, against the twelve years of destruction? For every such transcendent experience there were thousands of banal ones. The day-by-day "banality" of people being reduced to Mussulmen, dehumanized, and destroyed. Is it "mystical" to expire in a gas chamber? or to be shot down at the Black Wall of Auschwitz? or burned alive in a ditch?

And yet it would be unfortunate if the significance of this incident were minimized. For prior to its occurrence, Frankl had despaired that his suffering was meaningless. He and his fellow prisoners were clad in rags; they stood hacking away at the icy ground; gloom enveloped him, and he felt that death drew near. Altogether, the moment was no less grim than the one in which Camus's Sisyphus finds himself before his decision to keep rolling a stone up the hill. Precisely then, when his suffering was at a nadir, Frankl came to reflect on an image of his wife. And while he was "conversing silently" with her, he heard a "Yes," as though in response to the question: Is there any meaning to all this?

A moment later, as though to indicate some sign under the "miserable gray" sky, a light went on in a distant farmhouse. The "Yes" and the light were immediately followed by the appearance of the bird. All these "responses" to Frankl's question served to shape his belief in an ultimate higher meaning of human existence; and he felt he had found a "why" to live for.

As Frankl's inner life became more intensely attuned to memories of his wife and to the spiritual needs of his comrades, he apparently became more open to the beauty of the physical world beyond the barbed wire. On one occasion he was moved by a view of the mountains of Salzburg with their summits glowing in the distance. Another time he was arrested by an especially beautiful sunset.

> One evening, when we were already resting on the floor of our hut, dead tired, soup bowls in hand, a fellow prisoner rushed in and asked us to run out to the assembly grounds and see the wonderful sunset. Standing outside we saw sinister clouds glowing in the west and the whole sky alive with clouds of ever-changing shapes and colors,

from steel blue to blood red. The desolate grey mud huts
provided a sharp contrast, while the puddles on the muddy
ground reflected the glowing sky. Then, after minutes of
moving silence, one prisoner said to another, "How beautiful the world *could* be!" (P. 39.)

Here the sky was as a light shining through the darkness, and
the peacefulness and beauty of nature appeared to him as
evidence of the essential health of the universe.

The astonishing capacity of human beings! The prisoners
were hungry and cold, plagued by illness, harassed by guards,
and yet they would respond powerfully to a sunset, the song
of a lark, a flowering meadow.[19] In reflecting on this capacity
for such response, one begins to follow Nietzsche's words—
"That which does not kill me makes me stronger."

Ultimately, then, Frankl came to see his ordeal in Auschwitz
as a spiritual challenge that he wanted to be "worthy" of. Determined to "get through" [20] and not to "go around" his suffering,
he, in effect, said to himself: This apparently is how my lot
must be for a time; it is important to be of good courage.

When a man finds that it is his destiny to suffer, he will
have to accept his suffering as his task; . . . the fact that
even in suffering he is unique and alone in the universe.
No one can relieve him of his suffering or suffer in his
place. His unique opportunity lies in the way in which he
bears his burden. (P. 78.)

He had come to view his imprisonment not as something
abnormal, tangential to his existence, but rather as a spiritual
test—a test that had to be squarely confronted with toughness
of mind, compassion for the anguish of one's comrades, and
trust in the ultimate meaning of the ordeal.[21] In the face of all
that was Auschwitz, the will to believe that something significant might be taking place within oneself was an extraordinary
expression of spiritual freedom, and within this perspective,
Frankl's experiences as a prisoner are instructive for contemporary readers who wish to probe the moral center of Holocaust
literature.

It is important to point out the spiritual resistance of survivors like Frankl. It is well to realize that there were men in the camps who lifted up their fellow sufferers, who were moved by sunsets, the sight of flowers growing beside barbed wire. Although we have mountains of evidence documenting what was destroyed during the twelve Hitler years, we are far from glutted by accounts, like Frankl's, of the ways in which men remained impressively human.

But—and this is a big word here—just as it is important to know that some prisoners could not be spiritually broken by their imprisonment, so, too, it is well to realize that we have been discussing an exceptional man; few are capable of Frankl's iron-willed resolve—and ability—to conduct himself with dignity and courage in Auschwitz. Almost at the poles from Frankl's affirmative, will-to-meaning perspective is a view which has been preeminently represented by Primo Levi, the celebrated Italian-Jewish writer, in *If This Is a Man:*

> We do not believe in the most obvious and facile deduction: that man is fundamentally brutal, egoistic and stupid in his conduct once every civilized institution is taken away, and that the Häftling is consequently nothing but a man without inhibitions. We believe, rather, that the only conclusion to be drawn is that in the face of driving necessity and physical disabilities many social habits and instincts are reduced to silence. (P. 79.)

". . . many social habits and instincts are reduced to silence." What exactly is meant here? *What* social habits did Levi see "reduced to silence" in Auschwitz? His observations therein began with his arrival at the camp in early 1944; he was then twenty-four. Overnight he found himself in a nether universe where blows, cold, hunger, and death were the order of the day. A year later he took stock of his circumstances; and no writer on the Holocaust has written a more somber statement on how such an experience alters a man.

This time last year I was a free man: an outlaw but free,
I had a name and a family, I had an eager and restless

mind, an agile and healthy body. I used to think of many, far-away things: of my work, of the end of the war, of good and evil, of the nature of things and of the laws which govern human actions; and also of the mountains, of singing and loving, of music, of poetry. I had an enormous, deep-rooted foolish faith in the benevolence of fate; to kill and to die seemed extraneous literary things to me. My days were both cheerful and sad, but I regretted them equally, they were all full and positive; and the future stood before me as a great treasure. Today the only thing left of the life of these days is what one needs to suffer hunger and cold; I am not even alive enough to know how to kill myself. (P. 130.)

Levi soon realized that to exist from day to day in Auschwitz, one had to make compromises with one's usual standards of ethics and morality. Prisoners were encouraged by the camp officials to feel that each man had to look after only Number One.[22] Their captors had taken almost everything away from them— their clothing, hair, and even their names; the Nazis often referred to them merely by the numbers tattooed on their flesh. Indeed, the only thing the Nazis could not take away from them was their resolve to hang on, as long as possible, to a sense of their own identity.[23]

In such circumstances survival often depended, Levi observed, on being cunning, selfish, ruthless; sometimes it depended, alas, on serving as an informer. To resist the pressures that turned the resigned into Mussulmen, one had to wear an inner armor that was resistant to pity and, above all, hope; for hope could be still another source of disappointment and pain. Rather, the imprisoned were constrained to become inwardly as hard as steel so that they would not break.[24] In Primo Levi's words:

One has to fight against the current; to battle every day and every hour against exhaustion, hunger, cold and the resulting inertia; to resist enemies and have no pity for rivals; to sharpen one's wits, build up one's patience, strengthen one's will power. Or else, to throttle all dignity and kill all conscience, to climb down into the arena as a beast against other beasts, to let oneself be guided by those unsuspected subterranean forces which sustain families and individuals in cruel times. (P. 84.)

Which is to say that the suffering of the prisoners did not make for saints; brutalized, starving men compromised their usual moral principles for a piece of bread.

The narrator of Elie Wiesel's *Night* similarly became aware of the necessity for "aberration" and "compromise" in Buna. He too encountered few saints behind barbed wire. The majority of his fellow prisoners were bowed down by their suffering until they were "cringing like beaten dogs." For how many men could have maintained their self-respect in a place where the starving fought each other—sometimes even a son against a father—for a few crumbs of bread? [25] Nor was Eliezer, the narrator, himself free from "aberrations." When, for example, his father was struck by a Gypsy, Eliezer said nothing, did nothing. To have avenged the insult to his father by striking the Gypsy would have been a blow for his self-respect, but it also would have cost Eliezer's life. Again, when his father lay dying and with his last breath called for him, Eliezer admits he did not reply, fearing to draw attention to himself from camp officials;[26] moreover, he was relieved to be freed of the "dead weight" burden his ailing father had become for him.

> . . . at the same moment this thought came into my mind: "Don't let me find him! If only I could get rid of this dead weight, so that I could use all my strength to struggle for my own survival, and only worry about myself." Immediately I felt ashamed of myself, ashamed forever. (P. 108.)

But if he had been relieved of a "burden," not so of guilt. "I abandoned him"—this is the self-accusation that would never leave him.

Thus in the world of the Lager, where men had to be "less than human," where aberration and compromise were the rule, not the exception, where men found it wise not to try to "understand" what was happening to them, certain traditional social habits and values were, of necessity, "reduced to silence." Within this perspective, then, Levi poses the question, "Would it have made sense for a prisoner to adhere to a well defined and structured system of ethics and morals?" His answer is in the negative. What the world outside the camp considered virtue was not desirable from Levi's viewpoint or from that of his fellow prisoners. In the Lager the words "good," "evil," "just," and "unjust" lost their familiar meanings; Auschwitz and Buchenwald were hardly ideal settings for maintaining moral absolutes. If ever there was a time and place when the practice of an ethical relativism or situational ethics could have been justified, it was in the Lager.

The question bitterly raised by Levi at the end of his narrative is—"Are these, the survivors of Auschwitz, actually *men?*" The last chapter describes the miserable conditions confronting Levi and his comrades after the Germans had fled and while they were waiting for the Russians to arrive. Everywhere, prisoners, "starving specters," "unshaven with hollow eyes, greyish skeleton bones in rags" lay dying from typhus, pneumonia, scarlet fever, dysentery, and tuberculosis. Allied bombs had cut off the water and electricity supplies. Latrines were overflowing, for no one had the strength to look after their maintenance. During below-zero weather, the central heating system was inoperative and windows were broken in some of the huts. Even those who were comparatively well felt inert and helpless. Levi saw "ragged, decrepit, skeleton-like" prisoners dragging themselves over "the frozen soil, like an invasion of worms." Many corpses lay exposed in the snow; and others, "rigid as wood," rested on bunks in the huts. In the wards of the camp infirmary, lying in frozen excrement, patients continually cried out for help that could not be given to them. Some men died slowly, torturously, and in the grip of delirium. Levi describes one such death, that of a fifty-year-old Hungarian chemist.

Following a last interminable dream of acceptance and slavery he began to murmur: "Jawohl" with every breath, regularly and continuously like a machine, "Jawohl," at every collapsing of his wretched frame, thousands of times, enough to make one want to shake him, to suffocate him, at least to make him change the word.

I never understood so clearly as at that moment how laborious is the death of a man. (P. 155.)

I have deliberately underscored the details of the misery that gripped Levi and his comrades as they waited some ten days for the Russians to arrive. Perhaps it would be well if these details were to be repeated again and again, like the words of a dirge, for they are emblematic of the anguish that men inflicted upon men in our time. The post-Auschwitz reader who was not "there" feebly tries to imagine how it must have been during that period of waiting. How the prisoners must have lain in their bunks, wondering whether they could hold on until the Russians arrived. Some may not have wanted to think too much about the promised liberation, because hope could turn to unbearable disappointment and fresh pain. Supposing the Germans staged a successful counterattack, stopped the advancing Russians, and came back to the camp? So then one morning they would awake to see that the watchtowers were again manned by Germans.

It is not too surprising, then, that in such an inferno some would prefer death to life, like the former woman prisoner at Auschwitz referred to in the first chapter, the one who was found hiding among the bone piles of the dead in a barracks. After having been witness to the most degrading scenes of the twentieth century, many prisoners did not want to return to the "civilized" world. Enough! they must have cried out from the depths of their agony and given up the fierce daily struggle for clinging to life. Untouchables in their own eyes and in the eyes of others, they may have eventually looked to death as a merciful deliverer.[27]

And yet here one recalls Frankl thinking lovingly of his

wife while working, on a winter dawn, in a ditch. The ground
is icy, the guard hurls insults at Frankl, but the latter is
sustained by dwelling on an image of his wife. By comparison,
it is a rare moment in Levi's *If This Is a Man* when prisoners
are actually shown thinking of their loved ones. The most
notable exception to this condition occurs once when Levi and
his hutmates have had an unexpected windfall—an extra portion of rancid soup and turnips. They eat, feel content, and
then only are "able to think of our mothers and wives, which
usually does not happen." Did not often happen when a
prisoner was starving, because then he barely had enough
strength to think about one thing—bread.

Given the nature of his experiences, there is wisdom and
courage in Levi's reluctance to reach for moral absolutes or
"transcending" experiences. Not for him discourses on "love,"
"meaning," "beauty." Perhaps his morality is the stark honesty
with which he documents the view that to survive in Auschwitz
one had to become *less* than human. For we recognize the
terrible clarity of what he says to us at the end of his book:
There is no "meaning" to be gleaned from this wanton destruction; it was all cruelly senseless. And that finally we were
liberated does not mean that we won a victory over our oppressors. In the end, though freed, we were defeated; in reality
the Germans, though vanquished, emerged the victors. They
"won" because by the time the day of liberation came, we had
already been reduced to the state of animals. Hence the tone of
what must be one of the most profoundly disquieting passages in
Holocaust literature.

> We lay in a world of death and phantoms. The last
> trace of civilization had vanished around and inside us.
> The work of bestial degradation, begun by the victorious
> Germans, had been carried to its conclusion by the Ger-
> mans in defeat.
> It is man who kills, man who creates or suffers injustice;
> it is no longer man who, having lost all restraint, shares
> his bed with a corpse. Whoever waits for his neighbor

to die in order to take his piece of bread is, albeit guiltless, further from the model of thinking man than the most primitive pigmy or the most vicious sadist. (P. 150.)

There can be no more tragic commentary than Levi's on what was done by men to men in our time. When the prisoners pounced like beasts upon the bread that was given them, their liberators could not have readily pictured that these half skeletons had once spoken of Truth and Beauty, Goodness and Justice. So, too, in describing the liberation at Buchenwald, Eliezer of Wiesel's *Night* bitterly laments: "Our first act as free men was to throw ourselves onto the provisions. We thought only of that. Not of revenge, not of our families. Nothing but bread."

The liberated had come through cold, starvation, torture, and yet, in any ultimate reckoning, they had not really been freed. Many would long be enchained by recurring feelings of guilt and shame for having survived. Survived? In body, yes, but internally they would still be back in the camps. Hence the next to last sentence of *Night,* when Eliezer first looks at himself in a mirror after the Buchenwald liberation: "From the depths of the mirror, a corpse gazed back at me." [28]

That survivors like Levi and Wiesel cannot forget should not be surprising. If Anatoly Kuznetsov, who was never in a concentration camp or walled ghetto, fell into a "comatose state of endless nightmares" [29] when he began to write his novel on the mass murders at Babi Yar, how much more reason there is for those who were imprisoned behind barbed wire to be haunted by the past.

Bodies in calcium chloride, infants killed by lethal injections and placed in boxes, prisoners sharing their bunks with corpses, prisoners stealing bread from the sick and dying—this is what some of the survivors remember, looking back on their days in the camps. By contrast, Frankl remembers how his comrades and he responded to sunsets, to the singing of Italian arias. How, following his liberation, he walked through the country for

miles, hearing the joyous sounds of larks; and that at some
point during this walk he looked up at the sky and then went
down on his knees, thinking: "I called to the Lord from my
narrow prison and He answered me in the freedom of space." [30]
Frankl's rebirth in the fields needs to be valued for what it says
about the capacity of human beings to weather despair and loss
and still seek spiritual resurrection.

But saying that much is not to stipulate that Frankl's religious
experience ought to call forth from the reader an entirely affirmative response; his spiritual achievement here has to be seen in
scale. For, surely, the center of Holocaust literature is not concerned with a few remarkable men who may have transcended
their suffering but rather with the millions who were destroyed.
Resurrection may follow death, the phoenix may rise from the
ashes, but paeans of praise to human endurance and spiritual
resistance cannot turn ashes back into warm, living bodies.

Still, any balanced computation of the tragic facts must include recognition of some extraordinary ways in which the oppressed turned a human face to one another. Neither Primo
Levi nor Elie Wiesel, grim as their reports are, denies the crucial
importance of human relationships in the camps; indeed, they
point out that to the extent the prisoners helped one another
their ordeal was given a semblance of meaning. True, but not
the kind of meaning that evolved from meditating on an image
of one's beloved or from being moved by a sunset or from giving
a "pep talk" to one's despondent fellow prisoners; rather, the
meaning derived from responding compassionately to the needs
of one's comrades-in-suffering. Hence in *Night* the advice given
by a Polish prisoner at Auschwitz to newly arrived inmates:

> Let there be comradeship among you. We are all brothers,
> and we are all suffering the same fate. The same smoke
> floats over all our heads. Help one another. (P. 50.)

And when the veteran has finished speaking, Eliezer thinks:
"The first human words." [31]

In the last days of Auschwitz, Primo Levi, as we indicated

earlier, existed in a "world of death and phantoms"; starving prisoners waited to steal a piece of bread from the weak and defenseless; in the dispensary, the sick and dying lay beside corpses; the bodies of the dead rose out of ditches, latrines overflowed . . . Nothing in Dante's *Inferno* is more terrifying than these scenes in the Lager. Even so, embittered as Levi is by the knowledge of what men did to men during that time, the last words of his book describe the healing influence of human friendship. We see Levi and his friends Arthur and Charles by a stove at night, smoking cigarettes made of herbs, and listening to the sounds of gunfire in the distance. "In the middle of this endless plain, frozen and full of war, we felt at peace with ourselves and with the world." Sitting with his friends by the stove, Levi felt that they were beginning to change from Häftlings (prisoners) to men again. In Levi's words:

> Part of our existence lies in the feelings of those near to us. This is why the experience of someone who has lived for days during which man was merely a thing in the eyes of man is nonhuman. We three were for the most part immune from it, and we owe each other mutual gratitude. (P. 156.)

Giving to others—this, too, is the last word of Eugene Heimler's *Night of the Mist*. Heimler was twenty-one when the Germans invaded Hungary in the spring of 1944. His father was arrested and never seen again. His wife and family were deported to Auschwitz and died there. Heimler survived Buchenwald and other camps.

Before his imprisonment, Heimler felt—and apparently with good reason—that Hungarian Christians treated him, a Jew, as though he were a second-class citizen. Looked upon as an inferior person, he came to think of himself as one. Perhaps in an attempt to compensate for his frequent sense of being rejected by others, he became very competitive and sought to "show the world" that he was "twice as good" as those who looked down at him.

In Buchenwald he outgrew this immature need. There he

learned that he had to answer to no one but himself. From the beginning of his internment, he was thrown back upon his own resources; and the more these supported him the more he developed a sense of self-esteem. But before such awareness came to him, he was lashed by self-loathing. He felt shame in observing himself "scheming how to get a bigger chunk of bread." It shamed him also that he had become so hardened that even the "sight of people lying in their congealed blood in the ditch beneath the electric fence had ceased to quicken my pulse." He witnessed savage beatings when his fists were "no longer itching to get at the murderers." Nor was his self-esteem enhanced by the fact that he had become, in his own words, a "whore's pimp"; he made love to a Gypsy girl, and in exchange for his embraces she gave him bread, margarine, and jam.

What gave him a measure of self-respect was his determination to remain alive, to outlive his captors, so that one day he could bear witness against them.[32]

This resolve helped Heimler to "hang on" from day to day; and, gradually, as he came to see that he was being tested by Buchenwald, his inner strength was revealed to him. He discovered not only the positive values of his own life but also the deeper ways in which he was spiritually bound to other men.

> It was in Buchenwald that I learned, from Jews, Christians, Moslems, and pagans, from Englishmen, Serbs, Rumanians, Czechs, Frenchmen, Belgians, Dutch, Russians, Greeks, Albanians, Poles and Italians that I was only one more suffering insignificant man. . . . I learned that within me, as in others, the murderer and the humanitarian exist side by side; the weak child with the voracious male. That I am not in any way superior, that I am not different from others, that I am but a link in the great chain, was among the greatest discoveries of my life. (Pp. 158–159.)

In time, having come to accept his own worth as a man, he was able to accept the worth of others and to feel responsible for their warfare.

How, then, did he transform this recognition into deeds, a readiness to help others? In one instance he helped an old man. The man and Heimler were among a group of prisoners who had been forced to evacuate Buchenwald as the liberating Allied armies advanced. During the enforced march, the prisoners were deprived of food for three days. When finally the guards doled out a portion of boiled rice, the old man was too weakened to fight for a place in the queue. Heimler intervened, fighting off other prisoners, who had become like wild beasts at the sight of food, until a place was made for the old man. Concluding his account of that incident, Heimler writes: "When the food was given out and my turn came I gave the first plate to him, and not until I had watched him licking it clean as he sat by the roadside did I eat my own food."

In another instance, he elected to be the protector of sixteen young boys who had been brought to Buchenwald. Heimler probably saved their lives—but for his intervention, they very likely would have gone to the gas chambers—by getting permission from an SS officer to let them peel potatoes in the camp's kitchen. Working with these children before the ovens, he would attempt to feed their inquiring minds. He would speak to them about "democracy, about the world we hoped for after the war—a world where one would have enough to eat and be able to roam the streets freely, where everybody would be able to think what he liked and say what he thought. . . ."

At night in the barracks, they would ask him such questions as "whether there had ever lived another Hitler who had destroyed other people by fiery furnaces"; and they wanted to know also about the "differences between Judaism and Christianity, and whether Jesus was really the Son of God." In being their teacher, Heimler felt the power of his humanity; and thus, by his actions, by his extraordinary moral force, he had earned the right to respond to the question posed by a fellow prisoner, Dr. Ekstein: "Tell me, on what does it depend whether a man remains a man?"

Heimler had resolved to survive so that he could bear witness, and finally one day the German guards were gone, fleeing for their lives before the advancing Allied forces. He was free. But at first the liberation was of the body and not yet of the spirit. He was too numbed, exhausted, to grasp the fact that he was really free. During his imprisonment he had died a thousand deaths, and now that liberation had finally come he was not ready to turn his face toward a new life.

Then one day he walked in a large field under a clear sky; a vast silence was above and around him, like the "silence such as there must have been before the days of creation, before the heavens and the stars and this chaotic yet law-abiding world were formed." What apparently happened in that moment is powerfully described by Heimler in one of the most mystical and moving passages in Holocaust literature:

> Then I began to cry. I fell down on to the deep brown earth and breathed in the smell of the fields, and it was good. And the silence was broken by the whisper of the wind, by the song of the birds and by the distant lowing of the cows in far-off meadows. Somewhere a dog was barking. And it was good.
>
> I was part of the world and of the present again, and my tears had meaning because I had lost everything except my life. I knew that all the people I loved were dead. I knew that the freedom I had gained would be difficult to bear, and that it would be long before I found peace once more. I realized that I should go on searching for love.

As he was lying in the field, a young girl came up to him. She appeared frightened, wanted to know what he was doing there. Then she saw the triangle of the political prisoner on his jacket and understood.

> She knelt down beside me in the field, and slowly, without either of us uttering a word, tears gathered in her eyes, and soon our tears were intermingled on the earth. Then she spoke again in broken German; "I love you." "I love you, too," I said. We gazed at each other, two young people unable to speak, but our hearts crying out to each other

in a language louder than words. Then we kissed—and
it was the first kiss of love I had received or given since
Eva had died. There was no desire of flesh in this kiss,
only desire of the soul, a pure desire for unity between
man and woman. It was the kiss of a long-lost sister, a
re-discovered mother, a wife who over the years has become part of oneself.

She went as she had come, but suddenly she stopped.
"What is your name?" When I told her she repeated it:
"Jancsi, Jancsi." Then she said "Yarnicsku" in Czech and
slipped away and I never saw her again.

But I returned from that field like a newly awakened
man who has just seen the world and knows that he is
part of it and belongs to it. I felt that the funeral of my
dear ones had begun, and I recognized the birth of my
freedom. (Pp. 187–188.)

Frankl speaking to fellow prisoners of his hut, attempting to
lift up their morale; Heimler in Buchenwald ministering to sixteen children; Frankl kneeling in the fields and offering thanks-
giving to God for his deliverance from the camps; Heimler's
mystical experience in the presence of the young girl. Compare
these scenes with the endings of *Night* and *If This Is a Man:*
Eliezer's corpselike face staring back at him in the mirror; the
accumulating bodies in Levi's hut.

Given these differences, how should one conclude this investigation? It would be comforting to end by paying tribute
to those prisoners who apparently were "worthy" of their suffering. But I doubt that ending on a bright note would be
appropriate. Still, one need not go to the other extreme by as-
serting that there are no lessons to be derived from the reading
of these accounts. Perhaps all that should be said is that almost
any man, even those with exceptional inner strength, could be
dehumanized. That resolution and courage did not necessarily
prevail against starvation, cold, disease, beatings. That even
thoughtful and intelligent men did not find meaning in their
sufferings or find them spiritually "challenging." And that many
who survived did so at considerable expense to their humanity.

There is perhaps one slim consolation: despite the general condition that each man was fiercely alone in the struggle for survival, some prisoners apparently drew sustenance from their kinship with others. Their captors had almost succeeded in turning them into animals but through the grace of those who ministered to their needs, or who were helped by them, they came to feel like men again. In so doing they recognized the value of Alyosha's words to the boys at the end of *The Brothers Karamazov:* "Help one another."

And yet there can be no truly substantive consolation. We may assume the instances of human goodness during the Hitler era; nevertheless, a hard light needs to be focused and kept on the suffering and loss and brutality. Men died by the millions, and words in memoriam to the spiritual achievements of a few remarkable men are as nothing against that indictment. Studies on the Holocaust cannot resurrect the dead. The communities they once comprised are destroyed. Many of the survivors are marked for life. Nothing can alter those tragic facts.

3

"To Save Alive a Whole World": Chaim Kaplan's Warsaw Diary

During the Holocaust the urge to record the tragic events of the time in diaries was so intense in Jewish communities that Emmanuel Ringelblum[33] was prompted to remark: "Everyone used to write in the ghetto, journalists, writers, social workers, teachers, young people and even children." [34] What accounted for their activity? The most immediate explanation is that they wrote out of a need to bear witness; they wanted a detailed record of that dark time preserved for future generations. To write for future readers was a profound expression of faith in a tomorrow, in the possibilities for a better world, even if the writers themselves realized they would not live to see it—and many of these diarists knew they would not survive the Holocaust, that the days of their individual lives were numbered. Yet they prayed that their accounts would fall into sympathetic hands and be preserved. For it deeply concerned them that their deaths should not be meaningless, and that their strenuous efforts and devotion in maintaining the diaries should not have been in vain. Impelled by the need to bear witness, they wrote under the most impossible conditions: while they were starving, with numbed fingers in unheated rooms or cellars, when they were abed with illness, when they were ready to drop from exhaustion, when they risked their lives because the keeping of such diaries was expressly forbidden by the German authorities. Their recording went on even when the fate of their communities seemed unalterably hopeless. In the deepest sense, then, these diarists, even while on the brink of destruction, gave the enemy as hard a blow as those who exercised other kinds of inner resistance. For the diaries in themselves were a great spiritual triumph of the will over Nazi corruption.

We will turn now to the achievement of one of the two most important diarists of Polish Jewry during the Holocaust, Chaim Kaplan.[35] Along with Emmanuel Ringelblum's journal on the Warsaw ghetto, Kaplan's diaries, written in Hebrew, constitute the most complete record of the tragic events in Jewish Warsaw from the Occupation in 1939 to the beginning of the deportations in 1942. Hebrew scholar and educator, Kaplan served as the principal of a Warsaw elementary Hebrew day school for some forty years. His wife and he perished at Treblinka. Some twenty years after the Warsaw ghetto was destroyed, Kaplan's diaries were discovered by Abraham I. Katsh of New York University and in 1965 they were published by The Macmillan Company under the title *Scroll of Agony*.

"Therefore, but a single man was created in the world to teach that . . . if man saves alive a single soul from the world, Scripture imputes it to him as though he had saved alive a whole world." This is one of two epigraphs fronting Chaim Kaplan's *Scroll of Agony*. Concerning this epigraph, I should like to suggest that by keeping a diary Kaplan helped preserve for us the extraordinary spirit of a whole world—the world of the Warsaw ghetto. What we now know about its spiritual achievements would have been hidden from the light had the war gone the other way; for then the murderers would have been the historians. As it is, men like Kaplan have given a voice to the struggles of Warsaw Jewry for survival. His tenacity and commitment as a diarist paralleled the powerful will to live of the ghetto populace. Still, during the early days of the Occupation his essential attitude toward the community was not a positive one. He had to overcome a sense of hopelessness, to travel full circle from skepticism to pride concerning the mettle of Warsaw Jewry; so the diary begins on a note of doubt and ends in praise. In what follows, I shall trace this direction in his chronicle.

September 1939. The victorious German army was approaching the gates of a devastated Warsaw, and Polish military forces were crumbling before the oncoming enemy. The besieged city ("Beautiful Warsaw—city of royal glory, queen of cities") was being laid to waste by bombs and shelling. Even more difficult times could be anticipated once the Germans entered the city—especially for the Jews, who would be the first to suffer. Kaplan did not delude himself, as did some of his contemporaries, that the Germans would conduct themselves as civilized men.

Meanwhile, in the face of a food shortage, people went about frantically searching for bread; and there was a frenzied, widespread compulsion to hoard. This condition so distressed Kaplan that he wrote on September 20, 1939: "Man had become an animal, concerned only with brute existence and fear of starvation." And he saw his own distress mirrored on the faces of friends.

> Mourning is on every face. As our prophet said, "The whole head is sick and the whole heart faint." There is not one family who has not endured a sacrifice of some sort, human or material. Many of my friends have turned gray. It is hard to recognize them. (P. 36.)

"Mourning is on every face . . ." Kaplan apparently sensed that the days of Warsaw Jewry were numbered. It would have been understandable had he felt paralyzed, inert. But already he had started a diary and resolved, no matter what would come to pass, to go on making daily entries in it. "I have made a rule for myself in these historic times not to let a single day go by without making an entry in my diary."

Then the Germans, looking healthy, well fed, and stronger than he had anticipated, entered the city. They struck terror into the hearts of civilian Warsaw. Many immediately felt shattered, and Kaplan was no exception.

I find it hard even to hold a pen. My hands tremble; I have lived through a catastrophe that has left me crushed and physically broken. And what is worse, even as I sit writing these lines, I am still not certain that the catastrophe is over. (P. 41.)

But continue to write he somehow did. On October 2, a day after the Germans occupied the city, he apparently was writing by candlelight, because water and electricity services had been turned off. He went on making entries even after the Germans confiscated his apartment, in which he and his wife had lived for twenty-four years. All those years they had devoted a labor of love to decorating and beautifying that apartment, and then, in "one confusing hour," the Germans took it over. His heart is heavy, but the next day, October 4, despite the fact that the loss of the apartment had been a staggering blow, he pens a lengthy entry on the hardships of others.

It did not take the Nazis long, less than two weeks after their entry into Warsaw, before they began oppressing the Jewish population with restrictive measures far beyond those which they imposed upon the Poles. Jews were pulled out of their dwellings and taken off to forced labor, their bank accounts were closed, their jewelry and property confiscated; elderly, pious men were hunted down in the streets and their beards sheared off. Children were separated from parents who had been taken off to prison.[36] Kaplan observed sadness "on every face and dumb fear in every heart"; and he added, "We are caught in a net, doomed to destruction." As his doubts about the Jewish community's chances for survival increased, he exclaimed in an agonizingly hopeless cry of protest—"Almighty God! Are you making an end to the remnant of Polish Jewry?"

Disaster to the community was coming, he feared, not only from the outside, from the Germans, but also from the dangerous weaknesses of the Jewish populace as well. He especially expressed concern that many Jews had begun to look at themselves and one another with shame, as though they were inferior beings. He was further disheartened by what he viewed as the

absence of collective responsibility in the community. And he
reserved some of his harshest words for greedy self-seekers,
brutally aggressive individuals, blackmailers and swindlers
whose disgusting practices contributed to an atmosphere of
demoralization. In those early days of the Occupation, it seemed
to him that the Jews of Warsaw did not have the spiritual
strength and courage of their ancestors.

> We do not have the spiritual strength of our forefathers,
> whose souls were tempered, and who in the midst of
> terrible privation did not forget their spiritual needs and
> sacrificed themselves for these things. In the face of the
> persecution which endangers our physical existence, we
> are ready to give up everything that has heretofore been
> dear and holy to us. (P. 74.)

In contrast to his condemnation of individuals, Kaplan paid
homage to his dear friend, Jakub Zajac. A man of superior
character and large generosity, Zajac, by his exemplary conduct,
moved the diarist to write:

> If Polish Jewry can bring forth such a person, it is a
> sign that within it there exists something of the very
> finest. (P. 76.)

And yet, directly after having so honored his friend, Kaplan
sharply concluded the entry on a bitter note:

> And thus was this precious soul rewarded: his wife and
> two daughters were killed by a bomb; his home was razed;
> his shop was burned; he was left without a loved one and
> without belongings. Everything was destroyed, everything
> was burned. He was left alone and childless. Only the
> skin covering his flesh remained. Is this the way the
> Almighty looks after His dear ones? (P. 76.)

"Is this the way the Almighty looks after His dear ones?"—
this Jobian[37] question reverberates throughout the diary.

Warsaw Jewry appeared doomed to perish, and yet here and
there some individuals hesitantly asked the question, "Can we

survive?" It was as though they were waiting for some miracle to alter their circumstances.

And then, gradually, a kind of miracle, a "turning," did occur. Within a community of despair and paralysis, Warsaw Jews of every affiliation, every intellectual, cultural, and political interest, slowly drew together. Kaplan noted this change on November 30, only some two months after the occupation of the city by the enemy.

> We live broken and shattered lives; lives of shame and dishonor; lives of suffering and grief. But the power of adaptability within us is miraculous. Conditions change—the mode of work changes too. We have drawn together within ourselves; we have shriveled and shrunk; we follow the advice of the prophet: "Come, my people, enter thou into thy chambers, and shut thy doors about thee: hide thyself for a little moment, until the indignation be overpast." (P. 86.)

Jewish unions began to operate soup kitchens, collect and distribute food, provide drugs, medical aid, and clothing for the needy. Hundreds of teachers who were out of work following the Nazi-enforced shutdown of Jewish day schools, staved off starvation by instructing small groups of children in their own quarters. Kaplan himself undertook to teach a number of pupils in his apartment. Commenting on this accommodation, Kaplan remarked with an air of philosophical detachment: "This is a temporary, transitory livelihood born of necessity, the child of adaptability." This remark underscored his emerging confidence in the capacity of the Jewish masses for survival. Not that Kaplan underestimated the intent of the Germans to destroy them, but he was hopeful that the enemy had misjudged the potential inner strength of Polish Jewry. And it is in this context that his entry of February 9, 1940, may be read:

> There is no remedy for the Jews but *"Krepieren"* [to die like animals]. But the Jews refuse *"Krepieren."* It appears to me that the Führer is mistaken, as were Pharaoh, Nebuchadnezzar, and Haman. (P. 118.)[38]

We have touched on some of Kaplan's observations concerning Warsaw Jewry. Now what of the "mighty" conqueror? How did the Germans measure up in the eyes of the diarist? Characteristically, they fight, tyrannize, murder. It is as though they can do nothing else, as though their behavior is not even deliberate but compulsively automatic. Not that Kaplan labels all Germans as evil; his antennae are receptive to the infrequent instances of the enemy's humane conduct. Hence he records (p. 60) the story of a German officer who on encountering a woman in the streets and learning that she was Jewish gave her a half loaf of bread. Another officer, hearing of a Jewish boy who was beaten by a German soldier, gave twenty zloty to a passerby with the request that they be turned over to the injured boy; and the officer added: "Go tell your brethren that their suffering will not last much longer!" One of Kaplan's friends who was seized for forced labor reported to the diarist that the supervisor said to him: "Don't be afraid of me. I am not tainted with hatred for the Jews." Again, some German soldiers saw several Jewish boys playing a game in an empty lot, and asked to join them. The Jewish boys agreed, and Kaplan's concluding comment on this incident is: "After the game was over they parted like friends and comrades. It was a miracle."

A miracle precisely because such conduct on the part of the Germans was rare. More commonly, they acted as though the right to live was given only to the strong and not to the weak and defenseless, who became, in the diarist's words, "daily candidates for stoning, burning, beatings, strangulation, and all manner of unnatural deaths." Sometimes the cruelty of the Germans was so extreme that Kaplan was at a loss to understand it. On one occasion, having observed a "Nazi murderer" savagely beating a poor, elderly street peddler senseless, he writes:

> It was hard to comprehend the secret of this sadistic phenomenon. After all, the victim was a stranger, not an old enemy; he did not speak rudely to him, let alone touch him. Then why this cruel wrath! How is it possible to attack a stranger to me, a man of flesh and blood like

myself, to wound him and trample upon him, and cover his body with sores, bruises, and welts, without any reason?

How is it possible? Yet I swear that I saw all this with my own eyes. (P. 242.)[39]

Such brutality was possible because the Nazi did not allow himself to *feel* that the Jew, whatever the differences in his appearance, language, manner, or dress, was a human being. Not for the oppressor the Jewish injunction—Be kind to strangers, as you yourselves were once strangers in Egypt. It was much simpler to see the Jew as a thing, a vermin;[40] easier to snip off the beard of a pious, observant Jew in a frock coat than to think about the man behind the beard; easier to strike an unarmed man, to knock him down, kick him in his ribs, than to pause and ask oneself—*Who* is this man before me? What are his origins? What were his parents and grandparents like? Because to ask such questions was to invite humanizing the victim. It would have taken only the most minimal kind of moral imagination for the bully to realize that his victim might have the same personal qualities—probity, idealism, courage— that the Führer claimed all true Germans possessed. Instead, it was easier to reduce the Jew to an "it." Besides, why should one feel remorse about what happened to Jews when the Führer himself had told the German people *all* that they needed to know about these dangerous, conspiring enemies of the Third Reich?

And the "dangerous" enemy, a man like Chaim Kaplan, how did he conduct himself in comparison with the conqueror? The Germans boasted of being brave soldiers, tigers on the battlefield. Their literature was full of references to the heroic, noble qualities of the Volk. Hitler spoke as though some higher providence was supporting the Third Reich in a holy war. The lives of soldiers had not been lost in vain, for they had died in service of the Fatherland. Consider such patriotic bathos with the calmly rational antiwar sentiments of Kaplan:

Thousands of men are dying every day on the fields of death in Flanders. Let us speak the truth: Their deaths have no reason. Just as there was no reason for the deaths of the tens of billions who went before them. Every war is a senseless activity and its participants are, in my eyes, common murderers; when they die it is a pointless sacrifice. Let the slogans about the death of heroes be recited—these have not the power to make the crooked straight. (P. 159.)

And Kaplan concludes the entry with this statement:

I say that this attitude toward the casualties of war is a punishment for the national heroes who call common murder valor. I am the grandson of Isaiah the prophet, and I am at one with my ancestor in that bloodshed is abhorrent to me, in any form whatsoever. You may say that this is cowardice. I am not ashamed of that despicable quality. (P. 159.)

So spoke the "conspiring" Jew who was bent on world domination.

The "heroic" German rattles the saber, shoots pregnant women, and shatters the skulls of infants, while the "cowardly" Jew sits at a table assiduously making entries in his diary, insisting on absolute accuracy. "Every entry is more precious than gold, so long as it is written down as it happens, without exaggerations and distortions." (P. 58.) At the pain of death (because diary-keeping was forbidden by the Germans), Kaplan took it upon himself to record the suffering of his people in the hope that this record would reach future readers. "My heart is confident that these are the facts and that a future historian will find material here that may be relied upon, not just stories of the imagination." (P. 58.) Even through the darkest days, Kaplan commanded himself to write, as witness the entry of May 2, 1940:

In a spiritual state like the one in which I find myself at this time, it is difficult to hold a pen, to concentrate one's thoughts. But a strange idea has stuck in my head since the war broke out—that it is a duty I must perform.

This idea is like a flame imprisoned in my bones, burning within me, screaming: Record! Perhaps I am the only one engaged in this work, and that strengthens and encourages me. (P. 144.)[41]

Thus the impulse that commanded Kaplan to record was linked to the will of the Jewish masses to live, *tzu iberlebyn*. And this symbiotic relationship is nowhere better reflected in Kaplan's diary than the time some of the ghetto children laughed into ridicule a Nazi who demanded that all passersby remove their hats in his presence. The children gathered around the Nazi bully and began removing their hats five, ten, a hundred and one times, while feigning a look of reverence on their faces. As Kaplan skillfully and with evident relish tells the story:

Every one of the mischievous youths so directed his path as to appear before the Nazi several times, bowing before him in deepest respect. That wasn't all. Riffraff gathered for the fun, and they all made a noisy demonstration in honor of the Nazi with a resounding cheer. (Pp. 153–154.)

Kaplan concluded his account of this incident by saying: "This is Jewish revenge!" But he might have substituted the word "resistance" for "revenge." For such laughter at a time when the Nazis wanted the Jew to remain on his knees was not only an expression of collective vitality but also a way of standing erect before his oppressors. And who else but the Jew, Kaplan asked, could have engaged in such laughter? And he believed that a people able to laugh in such terrible circumstances would be able to survive.

A nation that can live in such terrible circumstances as these without losing its mind, without committing suicide —and which can still laugh—is sure of survival. Which will disappear first, Nazism or Judaism? I am willing to bet! Nazism will go first! (P. 182.)

"Nazism will go first!"—so much of Warsaw Jewry's inner strength was suggested by that sentence, and this strength nurtured the community's hope for a future, a tomorrow. Every

flicker of good news, of rumor, encouraged the populace to believe that they would survive. They were particularly hungry for
news from the war fronts. People in the streets asked one another—"How are the Allied forces doing today?" "What have
you heard?" Any report of a Nazi defeat was medicine for the
soul. When the news from Africa at one point was good in that
the Germans had been driven back, Warsaw Jews were ready to
believe that the downfall of the enemy was at hand. Indeed their
characteristic hypereagerness to find good news prompted Kaplan
to comment in an ironic tone leavened with affection:

> Jewish faith is marvelous; it can create states of mind that
> have nothing to do with reality. Like the believing Jewish
> grandfather who in anticipation of the Messiah always wore
> his Sabbath clothes, so we too await him. . . . And the
> news from Reuters always contains a certain intonation
> of expression to satisfy and comfort a spirit thirsting for
> a speedy and quick redemption. A stubborn people! (P.
> 287.)

A stubborn people indeed! They were convinced that their
tradition as a people exhorted them ("Therefore choose life!")
to stay alive. In the words of Dr. Saul Esh: "The Jews of Eastern
Europe felt in fact that victory over the enemy lay in their continued existence, for the enemy desired their extinction." [42]

This will to live persisted even when it became clear in mid-
November, 1940, approximately one year after the Germans had
entered the city, that the Jewish populace was trapped in a
closed ghetto. For at that time the Germans completed the
building of an eight-foot wall around the Jewish quarter. Thus
some half million inhabitants, many of them refugees from rural
communities outside Warsaw, were wedged into an area of
some 100 square blocks and 1500 buildings. Guards were
stationed on either side of the wall, sealing off the quarter from
the rest of Warsaw.

In the year since the Occupation, the enemy had not changed.
He continued to be the sadist, pillager, killer, pervert. On one

occasion, young Jewish men and women were brought to a rural bathhouse and "forced into imitating the sexual behavior of animals." And for a bizarre twist, the Nazis invaded the cemetery and ordered some Jews to do a Hasidic dance around a "basket of naked corpses." No wonder, then, that the sense of imminent terror ("A knock at the door after six o'clock," writes Kaplan, "is an evil omen which frightens you to the core") was everywhere.

But if the Nazis remained the same, Warsaw Jews, in Kaplan's eyes, were more and more impressive. In the early days of the Occupation, the paralysis of the populace had angered and depressed him. But even as the Nazis tightened their death hold, Warsaw Jewry drew together into self-contained networks of effective self-aid groups (e.g., house committees,[43] courtyard committees,[44] Zionist youth units). Kaplan especially praised the success of self-aid groups in planting and cultivating patches of gardens[45] on the sites of bombed-out houses, the backs of dusty courtyards, and abandoned lots between houses. In such places, benches and deck chairs were installed, and here children came to play, the elderly and invalids to sit and enjoy the sun or a view of the sky which might remind them of "the open spaces of the burgeoning world of nature outside the wall."

Almost everything was forbidden the people of the ghetto and yet, Kaplan marveled, they began finding ways to maintain a sizable degree of Jewish life. The German Command forbade public meetings[46] without its consent, but the people, knowing that such consent would not be given, held them anyway. One meeting, which particularly impressed Kaplan, paid homage to Theodor Herzl and Hayiim Bialik. "Gatherings of this sort don't enhance knowledge," he writes, summing up his impressions of the affair, "but the custom persists, and that is the important thing." The "important thing" was that identification with Jewish life be sustained.

Kaplan was further heartened by the ways in which the ghetto populace celebrated Jewish holidays. With a sense of wonder he referred to hundreds of minyanim that were held secretly during the 1940 High Holy Days. Worshipers prayed within inside rooms of tenement buildings; and in order to circumvent being heard by the Germans, they whispered their prayers and dispensed with cantors or choirs. People visited one another, exchanged greetings and cards, almost as in the days before the German Occupation. Similarly, a joyous Simhat Torah celebration is described in Kaplan's entry of October 25, 1940.

> In the midst of sorrow, the holiday of joy. This is not a secular joy, but a "rejoicing of the Torah," the same Torah for which we are murdered all day, . . . for which we have gone through fire and water. . . .
>
> . . . We have not shamed our eternal Torah. This was not a raucous celebration, but an inner one, a heartfelt joy, and for that reason it was all the more warm and emotional. Everywhere holiday celebrations were organized, and every prayer group said the wine blessing. The Hasidim were even dancing, as is their pious custom. Someone told me that on the night of the holiday he met a large group of zealous Hasidim in Mila Street, and they sang holiday songs in chorus out in public, followed by a large crowd of curious people and sightseers. Joy and revelry in poverty-stricken Mila Street! When they sang, they reached such a state of ecstasy that they couldn't stop, until some heretic approached them shouting, "Jews! Safeguarding your life is a positive Biblical commandment; it is a time of danger for us. Stop this." Only then did they become quiet. Some of them replied in their ecstasy: "we are not afraid of the murderer! The devil with him!" (P. 214.)

The public celebration of Hanukkah was also forbidden by the Germans. But this edict apparently did not stop the community from holding hundreds of parties in tenement rooms with drawn shades. And the December 26, 1940, entry mirrors Kaplan's pride in commenting on these celebrations. "Never before in Jewish Warsaw were there as many Hanukkah celebrations as in this of the wall. . . . Polish Jews are stubborn;

the enemy makes laws but they don't obey them. That is the secret of our survival." (Pp. 234–235.) So, too, a few months later the "stubborn" populace participated in lively Purim celebrations. Kaplan was among the celebrants at the Zionist soup kitchen on Zamenhof Street, and he writes about the warm holiday atmosphere in this popular social center:

> When we come here we forget our troubles and all the terrible events taking place outside. Here you can hear debates and sermons, arguments and quarrels as in the good days. And when your throat is dry you can wet it with a glass of black coffee without sugar.
>
> This year we read the Scroll in the Sephardic pronunciation; then we sang the holiday songs accompanied by a piano, and between one number and the other we even had a bite—three pieces of bread spread with butter, a taste of the traditional poppy-seed tarts, and a glass of sweetened coffee. (P. 256.)

How amazing! One can imagine that the faces of these celebrants were drawn, stretched tight from hunger and anxiety. And yet they sing! Despite what they had suffered since the German Occupation, they were still *there,* enduring, struggling, resisting the efforts of the Nazis to break them as a community. In witnessing such evidence of national kinship, Kaplan was moved to praise his fellow Jews; their suffering, he felt, had ennobled them:

> There is a well-known folk saying: "A worm that lives in a horseradish thinks that it is sweet." We have been like prisoners since the time we were pushed into the ghetto. The life of captivity, the yoke of edicts which never cease and are daily renewed, the degradation which has been our daily fare, the poverty and depression which grow as the sources of sustenance are cut off—the whole martyrology which is devouring us on every hand, and which has reduced us to objects of contempt unworthy of being thought of as men even in our own eyes—these things have made us into possessors of noble virtues; into people

who are hurt but do not strike back, who hear themselves
disgraced but do not react; and most of all, into people
who are content with little. (P. 314.)

Inspired by the struggle of Warsaw Jewry to survive, Kaplan
continued to write in his diary. And given his sense of responsibility to Jewish historiography, he would feel conscience-stricken
whenever it was necessary for him to put aside the recording even
for a brief time. Hence during one period, after a few days had
passed without an entry, he writes: "The spirit of dedication
which had left me in my moments of spiritual agony returns, as
though some hidden force were ordering me: Record!" (p. 233).

This, then, is the heart of the matter: his tenacity as a diarist
had its counterpart in the struggles of Warsaw Jewry to survive.
And it is in this perspective that Kaplan's commitment to his
diary may be seen as an extraordinary triumph of spiritual
resistance.

Still, it would have been asking for the impossible to expect
the ghetto populace to hold on indefinitely, staving off despair
and demoralization. For three years, since the beginning of the
war, what had sustained the community through days of excruciating sorrow and crushing hardships was the hope that the
Allied armies would defeat the Germans. But in the spring and
summer of 1942 this possibility waned. If anything, the German
military forces seemed to be growing stronger. Rommel was on
the move in Africa, threatening Alexandria and pursuing the
retreating British; Sevastopol had been reported captured;
America had not yet made its strength felt on the battlefront;
the Second Front was still only a rumor. The people of the
ghetto felt abandoned by the Allied world. They felt doomed.

All the while, terror and destruction within the walls increased. By day scores of people were arrested, often without a
word of explanation, and taken off to Pawiak prison for
execution. By night the Nazis would drag Jews out of their
flats and shoot them in the streets. Children and adults continued
to fall from hunger, disease, unendurable grief. Hence three of

the blackest sentences in all of Kaplan's entries: "Death lies in every street. The children are no longer afraid of death. In one courtyard, the children played a game tickling a corpse." The situation in the ghetto so rapidly deteriorated that by midsummer of 1942 Kaplan seemed resigned to the probability that he would perish without witnessing the defeat of the enemy.

And then, on July 22, 1942, the worst of the community's fears were realized. What heretofore had been a chilling rumor —that the Nazis were planning a mass expulsion of the populace to the East—became a fact. The German Command publicly announced that the majority of the population would be "eligible" for the transport almost immediately. Clearly, the end was in sight.

The announcement stunned Kaplan. Deportation would mean —he clearly understood this then, even without being apprised of the Final Solution—death. He himself was especially vulnerable, because apart from his being in his early sixties and his lack of experience as a skilled laborer, he did not possess the all-important *Ausweis,* a certificate guaranteeing, at least temporarily, immunity from expulsion. Thus, on the day of the deportation order, Kaplan's morale descended to a nadir.

> I haven't the strength to hold a pen in my hand. I'm broken, shattered. My thoughts are jumbled. I don't know where to start or stop. I have seen Jewish Warsaw through forty years of events but never before has she worn such a face. A whole community of 400,000 people condemned to exile. (P. 319.)

Perhaps it would have been of some consolation had he known that in a year from then the Warsaw Uprising would take place. As it is, the last entries of the diary depict his despair over a community which "has been turned into an inferno." On the first day of the deportations, 6,000 people were sent off to the *Umschlagplatz.* On the second day close to another 5,000 were taken away. Kaplan's July 27 entry records an atmosphere of widening panic: "People are being hunted

down in the streets like animals in the forest. . . . The children,
in particular, rend the heavens with their cries. . . . Everyone's
staff of bread has been broken. From whence cometh our help?
We are lost! We are lost!"

"We are lost"—there can be no more heartrending cry in the
literature of the Holocaust. The people had been under severe
pressure for three years and yet had managed to hold on as a
community. Now all their superhuman efforts in exercising
self-aid and collective responsibility seemed to have come to
naught. Warsaw, a community of 400,000 people, was going to
its destruction. In the midst of such unendurable anguish, Kaplan
felt unable to go on, and his July 28 entry details his exhausted
condition.

> Never in my life had I known the pangs of hunger. Even
> after I was pushed into the ghetto I ate. But now I too
> know hunger. I sustain myself for a whole day on a quarter-
> kilo of bread and unsweetened tea. My strength is diminish-
> ing from such meager fare. At times I can't even stand up.
> I fall on my bed, but rest eludes me. I am in a state of
> sleep and am not asleep, of wakefulness and yet am not
> awake. I am plagued by nightmares. (P. 328.)

The final entries of the diary describe how entire streets are
blockaded, the residents apprehended and taken off to the
Umschlagplatz. Others, frantically attempting to elude the deportation police, run "from place to place like madmen." And there
are those who, fearful of being shot for not complying with the
deportation decree, go toward the transfer point voluntarily,
pathetically "carrying small bundles under their arms." As the
blockade approaches his block, Kaplan, starving, so weak that he
is unable to stand, waits within his quarters, feeling that his life
is "forfeit and suspended over nothingness." From his windows
he observes the "fear of death . . . in the eyes of the few
people who pass by on the sidewalk." At this point, on the
evening of August 4, 1942, as Kaplan and his wife are fearfully
awaiting eviction from their dwelling, the diary breaks off
abruptly. We know what happened next: the Kaplans were

deported to Treblinka. Thus came the end for this distinguished educator, Hebraist, and worthy human being. A highly respected member of the community for some forty years, he suffered the final indignity of being hunted down like a common criminal.

Is there a glimmer of light beyond the dark concluding pages of the diary? There is if one gives emphasis to the fact that up to the very end Kaplan continued writing, even though this commitment sometimes involved several recordings a day. "But why tax your limited strength," his friends questioned him. "Besides, what good will it do? We are doomed here. We will not live to see the Nazi downfall. And the chances are that your diary will not be preserved."

But Kaplan could not accept their arguments and pleas, and he would not silence his writing. Though he dreaded deportation, what troubled him most of all was the fear that the diary would fall into enemy hands. It seemed to him that his death would be meaningful only if his chronicle was preserved for future readers. During his last days in Warsaw, even as he was packing boxes and making bundles in preparation for the deportation, he cried out—and it is one of the most resolute lines in the entire diary: "My utmost concern is for hiding my diary so that it will be preserved for future generations. As long as my pulse beats I shall continue my sacred task" (p. 335).

Almost three years earlier, referring to the death of his friend, Reb Jakub Zajac, Kaplan had written: "Sometimes, from among tens of thousands of the ravaged, your eyes are drawn to a face which haunts you no matter where you turn, does not leave you alone, follows you like a shadow and disturbs your rest. It is hard to understand why this is so. But so it is. The tragedy of a particular individual disturbs me to such an extent that I find myself obliged to make a special mention of it" (p. 75).

What Kaplan said of his friend might accurately have been said of himself, a man of humane intelligence and integrity. The individual voices of Warsaw Jewry are stilled. But reading

Kaplan's diary, we hear the voice of a "particular individual" from that time and place. The death of this single man, with his surpassing gifts of character and mind and spirit, makes concrete our sense of loss over the destruction of European Jewry.

Kaplan once wrote: "Our forefathers . . . immortalized their sufferings in lamentations. . . . Who will write of our troubles and who will immortalize them?" His diary is in itself an answer to that question. For this scroll of agony and praise has helped preserve the soul of a destroyed community that now lives in us, the readers for whom Chaim Kaplan bore witness.

4

From *Night* to *The Gates of the Forest:*
The Novels of Elie Wiesel

Elie Wiesel is widely acclaimed as one of the most important and influential writers in the literature of the Holocaust. His books *Night, Dawn, The Accident, The Town Beyond the Wall,* and *The Gates of the Forest* have reached an international audience. He has received a number of literary prizes (the Prix Rivarol in Paris in 1963, the National Jewish Book Council Award in 1964, the Remembrance Award of the World Federation of the Bergen-Belsen Association), and he was the first recipient of the B'nai B'rith prize for "excellence in Jewish literature." In June of 1967, an honorary doctorate of letters was conferred on him by the Jewish Theological Seminary of America.

Yet despite such recognition, his work has been criticized on the grounds that it suffers from overstatement, rhetoric, sentimentality, and a lack of literary inventiveness. This criticism has its source in a critical view which asserts that writers on the Holocaust need to keep their "cool." The familiar prescription of those who espouse this position is for the writer to maintain an ice-cold, surgical detachment from his material. Supporters of the "cool" approach to Holocaust literature argue that the suffering and atrocities of World War II cannot be rendered by direct emotional involvement—indeed, to become too emotional is to risk, they warn, losing control over one's material —therefore, let the writer employ obliqueness, irony, wryness, casual wit, lunatic humor, and subterranean fantasy. In sum, their argument is that the horrors of the Holocaust can be made endurable to the reader only through the manipulation of literary artifice.

Hence some reviewers have reacted predictably to a writer like Elie Wiesel. A. Alvarez (*Commentary*, November 1964) judged Wiesel's *Night* a defective book because it fell back on rhetoric and overstatement. How much better, he argued, is Piotr Rawicz's *Blood from the Sky*, because there the writer uses "diversionary tactics to convey intensities which he could not otherwise express." Elsewhere in the article he praised Rawicz for finding "imaginative ways around the atrocities." Herbert Mitgang called *The Accident* "falsely melodramatic." Another reviewer, Theodore Frankel (*Midstream*, December 1964), concluded that Wiesel's novel *The Town Beyond the Wall* is spoiled by "overwriting, sentimentalizing, and a maudlin philosophy whose shallowness too often contrasts oddly with the terrible misery which evoked it." Joseph Friedman (*Saturday Review*, July 25, 1964) found the "parables and moralizing passages" of *The Town Beyond the Wall* "diffuse and lacking in narrative pressure," but he admired the nonrealistic aspects of the work, especially the "impressionistic opening sequence, a fragmented, hallucinatory abstraction." And Emile Capouya (*Saturday Review*, May 28, 1966), in reviewing *The Gates of the Forest*, remarked that Wiesel's "literary talent, in the narrow sense, is quite meager."

Such evaluations prefigure the complications that arise when the reader is called upon to function as a critic of Holocaust literature. For how is he to judge literary works in this area? Is he simply to look at them as products of the literary imagination? But given the extraordinary nature of their content, how is this possible? And even if it were, what criteria would one use in evaluating them as literature? [47] Should a book like, say, *Night* be subjected to the same kinds of critical standards one would employ for a Hemingway or Fitzgerald novel? Is one to insist that precisely because the content of Holocaust fiction is often macabre, the author has a special obligation to eschew overstatement? Is one to argue that because many of these works are boiling, raging with the compulsion to bear witness to a time of chaos and destruction, the author ought to enforce a logical, astringently formal structure upon his works—to make order out of rage? I believe that David Daiches has offered the most satisfying and valid response to these questions, especially as they apply to Wiesel's books. In a review (*Commentary,* December 1965) of *The Gates of the Forest,* he writes:

> It is impossible to discuss Wiesel's novels in the terms which one would normally employ in reviewing fiction. All his works are clearly autobiographical, directly or indirectly, and they represent a genuine and sometimes painful endeavor to come to terms with post-Auschwitz life. The problem they deal with is central in modern experience, so that we are continually led as we read to go beyond the novels to reflect on how we ourselves should think or feel on this issue. They are thus important documents of modern consciousness and as such they ought to command the widest possible audience. As for myself, I would go further and confess that I cannot tell and I do not care whether these are great novels. But they are certainly important evidence, great documents, dealing with something which must perpetually haunt everyone old enough to have lived through World War II.

Not so much as *literary* works but rather as important documents of modern consciousness—that is how David Daiches would reply to critics who raise the question of Wiesel's books, "But are they art?"

To return to the question of artistic distancing, a sufficient detachment between the writer and his work is necessary to fiction. But surely it is no disservice to art to approach such stories on the Holocaust with the kind of passion *directly* rendered by a writer like Wiesel. For such tales "writ in blood," can one not respect the writer who risks underdistance rather than the reverse? In any event, to argue that since the literal facts of the catastrophe are often unbearable, they must be altered and made acceptable to the literary imagination is a curious prescription. Rather why not insist that the services of art be employed to make the literal facts of the tragedy even *more* unendurable? Is, for example, *The Last of the Just* any the worse a book because the ending, when Ernie Levy and Golda go to their deaths in a gas chamber, is presented in a detailed, realistic manner, without recourse to the strategies and devices of the literary imagination? Instead of being concerned about whether the author has used "diversionary tactics" and "imaginative ways around the atrocities," "pro-cool" critics might be better advised to determine whether the work is, to cite again the words of David Daiches, "an important document of modern consciousness."

Apart from the question of artistic distancing, is it a service to the facts of the Holocaust to keep a spotlight exclusively trained on the grotesque and bestial aspects of human behavior? Whenever men were at their worst, whenever they were without compassion or understanding, this, one adduces from reading the "pro-cool" reviewers, is fertile ground for artistic invention. The assumption here seems to be that the literary treatment of the inhuman makes for far more interesting reading than a presentation of admirable human conduct. Indeed, it is as though these reviewers were highly skeptical that exemplary behavior in the camps or ghettos can be rendered without the writer's falling into sentimentality.

Now obviously the realm of the perverse and inhuman is an appropriate theme for Holocaust literature.[48] But it is too bad that these same critics have not pointed out the abundance of impressive human relationships that is recorded in this body of literature: the warm responsiveness registered between Viktor Frankl and his fellow prisoners (*From Death-Camp to Existentialism*); Eugene Heimler and the sixteen children he protected in Buchenwald (*Night of the Mist*); Micklos and Weinstock (*The Seven Years*); Primo Levi and an Italian civilian (*If This Is a Man*); Tania and Eva (*Tell Me Another Morning*); Henriques and Hirsch (*Breaking-Point*); and Daniella and Fella (*House of Dolls*). The abundance of these relationships in the camps and walled ghettos lends support to the belief sounded in the last lines of Camus's *The Plague*: "What we learn in a time of pestilence: that there are more things to admire in man than to despise."

Moreover, those writers whose characters attempt to climb out of the pit of degradation and bestiality often take greater literary risks than those whose characters and situations emphasize the grotesque and bestial in human behavior. It can be easy for the writer to be icily dispassionate in writing on the sadistic, unfeeling temperament of Nazis. Much harder and difficult it can be to delineate the attempts of prisoners to be "worthy" of their suffering. Much harder and difficult and risky it is for the writer to render the loss of faith in a young man (like the protagonist of *Night*) imprisoned within the absolute hell of Auschwitz.

So that if one puts some of the "cool" writers beside Elie Wiesel, they seem rather unsatisfactory. Wiesel's books are powerful, painful documents of moral force. They sear through the defenses of the reader and strike at him like blows. They can leave one hurt, depressed, even suicidal. At the least, they make the reader feel on his pulses the writer's agony and anger in writing on the recent past.

Granted that Wiesel, by explicitly probing into the moral center of Holocaust experiences, is immersed in an undertaking that certainly involves the artistic risk of being sentimental and rhetorical. However, I think it is ill-advised to raise the question of his works posed or implied by some critics: "But are they art?" Surely there must be standards, other than artistic distancing, obliqueness, etc., for judging such powerful documents of moral force. Wiesel is an important writer not by the rules of contemporary fiction but because his books excite us to intense reflection. Clearly, they have suggested some of the most crucial, if unanswerable, questions pertinent to the Holocaust.

From night (an infernolike atmosphere of suffering and despair) to a gate (the possibilities for individual redemption)

—that is the route taken by the narrator-survivors of Elie Wiesel's five novels. From the walls of a concentration camp to the openness of a forest, symbol of the marginal and conditional presence of purity in the universe. The gate? It is the door, the way, leading, hopefully, to redemption. But the problem is that there are many gates in the Wieselean world and for each seeker only one way is right. At any rate, Wiesel's protagonists are in search of *the* gate, and the essential movement and direction of the five novels is from the dark night of the soul *toward* —but not *to*—spiritual rebirth.

It is not an easy road; along the way there are many trials. For a time the archetypal protagonist-survivor of the novels considers the "gate" of suicide as a way out of his unhappiness; later he considers going mad to blot out his grief and shame as a survivor. The worst trials of all are those times when he sees himself as a cursed soul condemned to wander in a nether world without respite and without hope of ever finding redemption. Thus, within this perspective, the "right" gate is at the poles from the cycles of hopeless wandering.

While the protagonist-survivor is in search of his own gate, what is it he "does" along the way? Essentially, he confronts the questions: What is the meaning of the Holocaust? the meaning of the suffering that afflicts Holocaust survivors? They are questions no longer asked of God by the Wieselean survivor; not asked of Him because "God may be dead." Or, if not dead, then indifferent to the tragic fate of European Jewry. And yet the survivor needs to think that there is sense in asking the question, What is the meaning of such individual and collective tragedy? Because he feels if there is not even the semblance of an answer to this question, then life itself and the will to live are unworthy.

But over the course of the five novels, the Wieselean narrator does not come even close to answering such questions, with the possible exception of a brief moment in *The Gates of the Forest* when a Williamsburg Hasidic rabbi tells him that human suffering is God's way of testing man, and that man's responsibility is to withstand such trials, for "at the end of such suffering, God awaits us."

Prior to that moment, the narrator generally feels alone and isolated in a world without God. He has escaped being turned into ashes but looks at himself as a kind of cursed ghost wandering in a twilight world halfway between the Holocaust dead and the living of the present who do not want to hear his message.[49] The living do not want to listen because his presence disturbs and frightens them. This does not surprise him, for even in his own eyes he is a "poisoned messenger" from the realm of the dead; Auschwitz and Buchenwald are still *in* him. As the price for having survived, he is seared by guilt. Thus in *The Gates of the Forest,* Gregor, a survivor, thinks: "He who is not among the victims is with the executioners."

But if the Wieselean protagonist is haunted by ghosts, he ultimately resolves to fight them. Without such resolution and effort his journey in search of redemption would be lacking in tension. The fact is, however, that he does grapple with the demons of his past; and the degree to which he ultimately succeeds in partly exorcising them may be determined by looking at the endings of the first and fifth novels. In *Night,* on being liberated at Buchenwald, the narrator looks into a mirror, observing that "a corpse gazed back at me." Hence the last image of the first novel underscores a mood of despair and the book ends on a note of unqualified blackness; *Night* ends in night.

Now *The Gates of the Forest* hardly ends in light; the narrator is still an unhappy, tortured man. And yet the difference is this: in the final moments of the book, Gregor goes to a synagogue to recite Kaddish for his father who died in Buchenwald; and this act indicates an emergent openness to the possibilities for some future renewal of religious faith.

From Buchenwald to the synagogue, from the image of a corpselike face in a mirror to the grandiloquent and serene words of the Kaddish—these are the key beginning and terminal road markers along the route taken by the five novels. But of course this is to see them from an all-too-wide overview. What is needed—and what now follows—is a detailed examination of each of the five novels.

Night defines the nature and charts the consequences of a loss of faith in the protagonist, Eliezer, as incident by incident, layer by layer, his trust in God and man is peeled away. It is this "peeling down" process which constitutes the essential structure of *Night* and enables us to see it as a whole; the purpose of what follows is to adumbrate this process.

Eliezer as a boy in Sighet, a small town in Transylvania, absorbed the religious beliefs of his teacher, Moché the beadle, at a Hasidic synagogue. Moché prescribed that one should pray to God for "the strength to ask Him the right questions."

> "Man raises himself toward God by the questions he asks Him," he [Moché] was fond of repeating. "That is the true dialogue. Man questions God and God answers. But we don't understand His answers. We can't understand them. Because they come from the depths of the soul, and they stay there until death. You will find the true answers, Eliezer, only within yourself!" (P. 16.)

Later, as a result of his experiences during the Holocaust, Eliezer would cease expecting to get answers to his questions; indeed, he would come to say that question and answer are not necessarily interrelated. Then what should men do—stop asking such questions? Not at all. The protagonists in the later novels, in *The Town Beyond the Wall* and *The Gates of the Forest,* contend that men must continue to pose them. But not to God, who, in the eyes of the Wieselean narrator, remained silent during the Holocaust. Rather, these questions must come out of the depths of men and be addressed to other men. For to be human, to exercise one's humanity, is to go on posing such questions, even in the face of the Absurd, of Nothingness.

But such recognition for the protagonist was in the distant future. Meanwhile, in the beginning of *Night,* the boy Eliezer did not question Moché's teachings. He believed that as long as Jews studied and were pious no evil could touch them. The

Germans proved he was mistaken when they occupied Sighet in the spring of 1944. In consequence, the first of Moché's teachings jettisoned by Eliezer was the notion that a Jew should live lowly, be self-effacing and inconspicuous. Certainly Moché was an "invisible" man. The narrator says of him: "Nobody ever felt embarrassed by him. Nobody ever felt encumbered by his presence. He was a past master in the art of making himself insignificant, of seeming invisible."

And yet remaining "invisible" did not help Moché; the Germans systematically disposed of him along with Sighet's entire Jewish population.[50] In the beginning of the Occupation, Jews were ordered to wear yellow stars, then they were driven out of their homes and herded into ghettos. A "Jewish council" and Jewish police were imposed on them. Some of the populace desperately attempted to escape annihilation by stationing themselves in such places and at such tasks that would keep them out of sight. And they further deluded themselves by thinking: The Germans—after all, this was the twentieth century—would oppress them up to a certain point and no further. So the popular advice was: Just do what they tell you; they only kill those who put up resistance. But in the end, packs on their backs, the Jewish community was marched off to a transport center, jammed into cattle wagons, and sent off to concentration camps. Meekness, staying "invisible," had not worked. And it is as though Wiesel laments that here was another instance wherein the Jew contributed to his agelong fate as victim and "specialist" in suffering. Ought not the time come when the Jew will make history itself tremble—when, if need be, *he* will be the executioner? In sum, Eliezer learned from having undergone the Occupation and deportation, that it is useless to employ the disguises of the "invisible" Jew. And this recognition constituted the first major puncture of his heretofore innocent faith in the teachings of Moché.

Belief in God the fifteen-year-old Eliezer had before he came to Auschwitz. But there, in *anus mundi,* that faith was consumed in the flames that consumed children. There "God" was the official on the train ramp who separated life from death with a flick of a finger to the right or left. Yet some Jews continued to urge children to pray to God. "You must never lose faith," they said to Eliezer, "even when the sword hangs over your head. That's the teaching of our sages."

But could the sages have imagined the limitless depravity of the Nazis? Could they, in all their wisdom, have counseled a boy of fifteen on how to react to the mass burning of children? To see a child's head, arms, and legs go up in flame—that is an indisputable fact, a measurable phenomenon.

Did He care that children were being consumed by fire? This is the question raised by the narrator of *Night*. And if He does nothing to prevent the mass murder of children, Eliezer cries out: "Why should I bless His name?" This outcry is the sign of, as François Mauriac says in his foreword to the book, "the death of God in the soul of a child who suddenly discovers absolute evil." And this breakdown of religious faith calls forth Eliezer's resolve "never to forget."

> Never shall I forget that night, the first night in camp, which has turned my life into one long night, seven times cursed and seven times sealed. Never shall I forget that smoke. Never shall I forget the little faces of the children, whose bodies I saw turned into wreaths of smoke beneath a silent blue sky.
> Never shall I forget those flames which consumed my faith forever.
> Never shall I forget that nocturnal silence which deprived me, for all eternity, of the desire to live. Never shall I forget those moments which murdered my God and my soul and turned my dreams to dust. Never shall I forget these things, even if I am condemned to live as long as God Himself. Never. (Pp. 43–44.)

So, too, on the eve of Rosh Hashanah, Eliezer, who until then had always been devoted to this holiday, thinks, bitterly:

> Why, but why should I bless him? In every fiber I rebelled. Because He has had thousands of children burned in His pits? Because He kept six crematories work-

ing night and day, on Sundays and feast days? Because
in His great might He had created Auschwitz, Birkenau,
Buna, and so many factories of death? How could I say
to Him: "Blessed art Thou, Eternal, Master of the Universe, who chose us from among the races to be tortured
day and night, to see our fathers, our mothers, our brothers,
end in the crematory? Praised be Thy Holy Name, Thou
Who hast chosen us to be butchered on Thine Altar?"
(P. 73.)

After Auschwitz, Eliezer could no longer speak of God's goodness or His ultimate purposes.

What is the immediate consequence of this loss of faith? Eliezer feels as though he were a lost soul condemned to wander in
a haunted realm of darkness. Here the word "darkness" needs
to be underscored, for it is a world at the poles from the one of
"light" which Eliezer, as a student of the Cabbala and Talmud,
inhabited in Sighet. By day the Talmud, and at night, by candlelight, he and his teacher Moché would study together, searching for "the revelation and mysteries of the cabbala." There
was not only candlelight when they studied; the Talmud, the
Zohar, the cabbalistic books themselves *were* light; they illumi-
nated the nature of the "question" and suggested the answer;[51]
they seemed to draw Moché and Eliezer toward the shining realm
of the eternal "where question and answer would become one."

But the light in *Night* is of brief duration; the atmosphere
of the book is almost entirely that of blackness. The fires of
Auschwitz consume the light, the religious faith, of Eliezer and
leave him a "damned soul" wandering through a darkness where
question and answer would *never* become one.

What other kinds of disillusionment are experienced by
Eliezer? I have already pointed out two—his realization that
to be an "invisible" Jew did not protect one from the Nazis
and, second, his turning away from God on witnessing the mass
burning of children at Auschwitz. There was also his loss of
faith in both the myth of twentieth-century civilized man and
the tradition of the inviolable bonds between Jewish parents

and children. Before coming to Auschwitz, Eliezer had believed that twentieth-century man was civilized. He had supposed that people would try to help one another in difficult times; certainly his father and teachers had taught him that every Jew is responsible for all other Jews. Until the gates of a concentration camp closed upon him he had no reason to doubt that the love between parents and children was characterized by sacrifice, selflessness, and utmost fealty.

But Auschwitz changed all that. There he was forced to look on while a young boy was tortured and then hanged—his death taking more than a half hour of "slow agony." There dozens of men fought and trampled one another for an extra ration of food. In one instance, he saw a son actually killing his elderly father over a portion of bread while other prisoners looked on indifferently. In Auschwitz the conduct of most prisoners was rarely selfless. Almost every man was out to save his own skin; and to do so he would steal, betray, buy life with the lives of others.

Eliezer's progressive disillusionment did not come about simply because of what he witnessed in Auschwitz; he did not only observe the breakdown of faith; he himself in part caused it to happen. Consider Eliezer's thoughts and conduct with respect to his father when both were concentration camp prisoners. Eliezer feels that his father is an encumbrance, an albatross, who jeopardizes his own chances for survival. The son himself is ailing, emaciated, and in attempting to look after the older man strains his own limited physical resources. Moreover, such efforts make him dangerously conspicuous—always a perilous condition for concentration camp prisoners. And yet he despises himself for not having lifted a hand when his elderly father was struck by a Kapo. He had looked on, thinking: "Yesterday I should have sunk my nails into the criminal's flesh. Have I changed so much, then?"

Eliezer's conflict of wanting to protect his father and, conversely, to be separated from him, is so desperate that when the father is on the verge of dying, the son feels ashamed to think: "If only I could get rid of this dead weight, so that I could use all my strength to struggle for my own survival, and only worry about myself." Again, when the dying man is struck with a truncheon by an officer, Eliezer, fearing to be beaten, stands still, like one paralyzed. Finally, when his father is taken off to the crematoria, the son cannot weep. Grief there is in him and yet he feels free of his burden. Thus another illusion is discarded by a boy who had been reared in a tradition that stresses loyalty and devotion to one's parents.

The death of his father leaves Eliezer in a state of numbness; he feels that nothing more can affect him. But there remains still another illusion he is to shed—the belief that on being liberated the prisoners would be capable of avenging themselves on the enemy. They had endured so much in order to live to the day of liberation. How often had the prisoners spoken to one another about what they would do to the Germans. And yet when Buchenwald is liberated, Eliezer observes with anger and disgust that his fellow prisoners are concerned only with bread and not revenge.[52]

He has lost not only his father but also faith in God and humanity. Many of his previously untested beliefs in the staying powers of the "invisible" Jew, the unquestionable justice of God, the built-in restraints of twentieth-century civilization, and the enduring strength of familial bonds between Jewish parents and children have been peeled away. He will have to journey for a long time and through many lands before arriving at that point of retrospective clarity when he can even first frame the "right questions" concerning his season in hell. He will need to stand before some "false" gates before he can turn away from them. And yet, all through this time, he is to hold fast to the belief that his teacher Moché instilled in him: that there *is* an "orchard of truth," and that for entering the gate to this place every human being has his own key. One function of the Wieselean novels that follow *Night* is to trace the protagonist-survivor's journey in search of such a gate.

In *Night*, Eliezer was a boy of fifteen in Auschwitz. Elisha, the protagonist of Wiesel's second novel, *Dawn*, is a young man of eighteen in Palestine. Seeing himself as a messenger from the dead among the living, Elisha attempts to exorcise the past but cannot; neither can he give himself to the living; he continues to wander in an underground world between the living and the dead. Having seen God and civilized man "die" at Auschwitz, he has few illusions left—and yet he still maintains the slim hope that redemption may be ahead.

In the beginning of *Dawn,* Elisha, as a member of the terrorist movement in Palestine, seeks to be persuaded that if he places himself on the other side of the gun, he will be able to exorcise the "night" in his past. Never again does he want to be helpless before an oppressor. He would like to believe that by killing the enemy—in this case the English—he can exorcise memories of having been the victim during the Holocaust.

The man who urges Elisha to become an "executioner" is Gad, a leader in the terrorist movement. Gad considers himself a messenger from the future, and he wants Elisha's future; that is, he exhorts Elisha to fight for a Jewish homeland in Palestine. And the most direct way of doing this, Gad argues, is to strike terror into the hearts of the English occupying forces. He urges his fellow terrorists to hate the enemy and to let the latter be fully apprised of the depth and measure of this hate. An elemental hate which would be justified, Gad insists, because through its long history of persecution, the Jewish people have never learned to hate their persecutors, and they were kept in perennial bondage as victims. Until the Jew became the executioner, he would go on being the victim. Hate against the enemy now offered possibilities for a drastic alteration in the future course of Jewish history. Since God is dead, they, the terrorists, would take upon themselves His awesome power of separating life (in this case the lives of the English in Palestine) from death.

"On the day when the English understand that their occupation will cost them blood they won't want to stay," Gad told us. . . . "The commandment *Thou shalt not kill* was given from the summit of one of the mountains here in Palestine, and we were the only ones to obey it. But

that's all over; we must be like everybody else. Murder
will not be our profession but our duty. In the days and
weeks and months to come you will have only one purpose:
to kill those who have made us killers. We shall kill in
order that once more we may be men." (Pp. 29–30.)

The novel turns on Elisha's test of Gad's views. An English
officer, a Captain John Dawson, has been captured by the terrorists and condemned to be executed in retaliation for the
previous executions of Jewish resistance fighters by the British
—specifically for a Jewish fighter whom the British have lately
sentenced to death. Elisha has been ordered by the commander
of the terrorists to be the executioner; and the execution is to
take place at the same time that the Jewish fighter is scheduled
to be hanged in the prison at Acre. The English believe that the
Jews are bluffing, that they are not really prepared to go through
with the execution, to extract an eye for an eye. After all, the
British assume, aren't they long accustomed to turning the other
cheek? But this time the British have misjudged the new kind
of toughened Jew that had been bred and formed in the Yishuv
(community) of Palestine.

Elisha, however, is not one of those who were raised in
Palestine. His early years as a European Jew and his experiences
in concentration camps have marked him. As a boy he was
taught not to hate Amalek but merely to remember him; he
was instructed not to fight with Gentiles but rather to keep out
of their way. "Man should belong to the persecuted and not the
persecutors," he well may have read in the Talmud. And in the
camps he found it prudent to remain inconspicuous, "invisible."
Yet even as he girds himself for the task of executing Dawson,
he hears in the foreground of his consciousness the injunction:
"Thou shalt not kill." Not that as a member of the terrorist
movement he hadn't killed before; in the past he had ambushed
and shot to death English soldiers. However, then the English
had been armed, and at least they had been capable of firing
back. But John Dawson is helpless and Elisha, acting alone,
would have to look him in the eyes and pull the trigger. He fears

he might not feel enough hate to do this. And even if he did pull the trigger, would he not then become, in his own eyes, a kind of SS guard shooting down a defenseless prisoner? Moreover, it troubles Elisha that in killing Dawson he may be judged by the spirit of the Holocaust dead and found guilty; that is, found wanting by the moral and religious standards of his parents and former teachers. They would have enjoined him to be kind and merciful to others. They, who had been murdered by the Nazis, would have said that it is never justified for a Jew to become an executioner. And so, as the dawn on which he has been ordered to kill the British officer approaches, Elisha is haunted by the faces of the Holocaust dead.

Why do they judge me of all people? he cries out within himself. Had he not also been a victim, a prisoner in the camps? Had he voluntarily chosen to return from the kingdom of the dead bearing a poisoned message for the living? So why should he be judged? Rather let God be judged, He who had turned his back on the world of men.

But it is not only the dead, he recognizes, who judge him for having survived the camps or for having accepted the order to execute the English soldier; it is also his own silence. That is, his self-imposed alienation from the uncomprehending, "uninitiated" living who were not "there" condemns him.

Finally, when Elisha comes face to face with Dawson a short while before the dawn of the scheduled execution, his exposure to terrorist ideology is put to the supreme test. With this result —he finds himself unable to hate Dawson. Momentarily it appears he will not be able to go through with the execution. And even though he finally does kill Dawson, this act does not bring the young survivor to the promised new "dawn" that Gad had described; Elisha still remains in "night," still views himself as a corpselike messenger from the dead condemned to "wandering in the half world" of the living. Previously, he had hoped that by killing a man who was one of the enemy, he would put an end to his own cursed existence as a "messenger." He had allowed himself this thin hope, and now it too had collapsed. By killing Dawson he had entered a "gate"—only to find himself still lost in an interior wilderness. And just as at the end of *Night* Eliezer beholds a "corpse" on looking at himself in a mirror, Elisha discovers that a frightening "tattered fragment of darkness, hanging in midair, the other side of the window" is actually his own face. Darkness is the note on which the first two novels conclude.

There is still another "false gate" which the protagonist-survivor will enter in the third novel, *The Accident*. Thereupon he will learn that suicide is no solution for his anguish. Now it may be argued that suicide was a justified act for some prisoners of the death camps. Here one thinks of some inmates of Treblinka who took their own lives rather than endure further suffering. They stood up on chairs, attached belts to their necks and the ceilings of their huts and then kicked away the chairs. It was their way of exerting one of the few freedoms the Nazis could not deny them—the freedom of determining the nature and circumstances of their own deaths.

So, too, it is difficult to condemn the suicide attempt of Eliezer, the narrator of *The Accident,* who practically invited a taxi to strike him down while he was crossing a New York street. Why should he, a survivor, be expected to fight for his life, to hold fast to the Talmudic dictum—"therefore choose life"? For the facts are that Eliezer has suffered the loss of his parents, relatives, friends, all victims of the Holocaust. He has been disillusioned by God and man. And he feels guilt and self-incrimination for having survived.

But if Eliezer wants to die, the presence of Wiesel is clearly felt in the story, and he prefers that his protagonist live. To live, to die—it is out of these alternating pressures that the book receives its focal tension. We have already seen that the question "to kill or not to kill" generated tension in *Dawn*; and we will shortly observe that the central tension in the novel directly following *The Accident, The Town Beyond the Wall,* has its source in the protagonist's obsessive question—"to go or not to go mad?" It may be instructive, therefore, to examine the response of Eliezer to the question "to live or not to live?"

At the outset of the story, Eliezer is actually waiting for an accident to happen to him. In a sense he already has been slowly dying ever since his liberation from a Nazi extermination camp. His girl friend, Kathleen, tries, uselessly, to edge him out of his "sickness unto death." She would want him to enjoy the physical pleasures of the everyday world. Eat! she urges him; for it disturbs her that Eliezer has little interest in food. But what she wants for him, he does not want for himself; he is hungry for neither food nor life. Filled with self-disgust for having survived when so many who were close to him did not, he continually thinks of the dead. It is as though he wanted the dead to judge him, to find him guilty. Not the living, because they were not "there" and hence are not worthy to make such judgment. So if he does not owe the living explanations for his agony, neither need he address his "questions" to them, nor seek their counsel; before the living he need maintain only a silence. Or, perhaps better yet, remove his poisonous presence altogether from their sight by committing suicide.

It is at this point, when he is unable to respond to Kathleen's love or to her pleas to *choose* life, that the accident occurs.

After being struck by the taxi and suffering broken bones along the entire left side of his body, internal hemorrhage, and brain concussion, he nevertheless manages, miraculously, to live. A miracle like that other one wherein he survived Buchenwald. In both instances, following the accident and following liberation from the camp, he had been brought back to life from the edge of the grave; and in both instances he half resented having survived.[53]

His will to die stems not only from a sense of guilt at having survived but also from revulsion in seeing himself as a "poisoned" messenger. It is as though Eliezer assumes that by his very presence, he is a mirror to frighten others, to prevent them from forgetting what the Holocaust past was. He who once enjoyed the warm, familial atmosphere of the shtetl, especially as it was embodied in his pious, loving grandmother, now feels empty, cold, emotionally numb; and he believes that his very presence poisons in others the possibilities for joy and hope.

It is not only his "poisoned" presence, Eliezer believes, that frightens others, but also his messages, the stories he tells of the German Occupation, the long night in Buchenwald and Auschwitz, constrain his auditors, those who were spared his suffering, to interrogate their own lives. And indeed, at one point Eliezer says to a resident doctor following the accident:

> My legends can only be told at dark. Whoever listens
> questions his life. . . . The heroes of my legends are cruel
> and without pity. They are capable of strangling you.
> (P. 73.)

"Whoever listens questions his life"—this might well be an emblematic warning to readers of Wiesel's works. For his stories, probing the darker reaches of human experience, can profoundly disquiet the reader. Whoever turns to this writer can expect to have his most basic assumptions questioned. It is not simply that Wiesel asks such age-old questions as, for example, What is the meaning of suffering? Other writers could ask the same question and not at all affect the reader. Rather it is because of *who* he is, a man who has suffered beyond the scope or endurance of most men, that he poses such questions with searing, authoritative force.

But to return to *The Accident,* while Eliezer feels compelled to be the interrogator, there are those who seek to offer him, if not answers to his questions, friendship and love. For one, his girl friend Kathleen. She pits, unsuccessfully, the warmth of her affection against his defenses. The struggle between them generates the dialectical tension of this section of the book. Live! she exhorts when she pleads with him to eat. Live! she says with her body when they make love. But why live? he counters. Simply to eat another meal, to lie down for another few hours' sleep, to work yet another day? No, he would not—unless he could, like Tolstoy, following his suicide attempt during his fifties, find a moral sanction for life itself. But where is this sanction to come from? Certainly not from a belief in God, for where was He when twelve-year-old girls were forced to sleep with the SS? Nor from enduring suffering in the belief that it is a trial which strengthens and ennobles us. For on the basis of what he had witnessed in the camps, suffering often brought out the worst in people, made devils of them and not saints. Not for him Dostoevsky's view that one must be "worthy" of one's suffering.

While Eliezer, his broken body encased in plaster, lies in a hospital, Kathleen and the resident doctor persist in urging him to fight for his life. It is as though all three are characters in a medieval morality play where the forces of life are deployed against the forces of death. If Eliezer is not responsive to the efforts of Kathleen and the doctor, it is not because he distrusts or deprecates their motives. He knows them to be generously well intentioned; but, nevertheless, they are powerless to alter his fundamental condition of despair. Clearly, they want him to bury the dead within himself and turn his face toward the possibilities of the present. But Eliezer cannot forget the dead. Even if he could, even if he could settle for a "normal," satisfying life, sooner or later the past would pursue him with double vengeance, with so much force that he would risk going mad.

> "I think if I were able to forget I would hate myself [Eliezer says to Kathleen, speaking about his experiences in the camps]. Our stay there planted time bombs within us. From time to time one of them explodes. And then we are nothing but suffering, shame, and guilt. We feel ashamed and guilty to be alive, to eat as much bread as we want, to wear good, warm socks in the winter. One of these bombs, Kathleen, will undoubtedly bring about madness. It's inevitable. Anyone who has been there has brought back some of humanity's madness. One day or another, it will come back to the surface." (P. 105.)

Actually, Eliezer's prognosis of the prospects before him, if he wills to live, is convincing. A survivor like him might for a time be able to turn his back on the recent past and to impose on his daily life a patina of normalcy. To all outward appearances, such a person might seem to be ably functioning in his environment. The survivor might have the illusion that finally he is clear of the past. Then one day, perhaps twenty or thirty years later, he would be forced to turn and again confront the horrors of the Holocaust. And such confrontation might well result in madness.

But if Kathleen and the doctor are not successful in their efforts to convince Eliezer to "choose life," for a time it seems that his friend, Gyula, might be. The latter, a painter of Hungarian origin, has a vital, tough-minded temperament, and for Eliezer he is a "living rock." By contrast with his friend's sense of futility and resignation, Gyula actively chooses "to pit himself against fate, to force it to give human meaning to its cruelty." For Gyula, what a man must do is clear: God died during the Holocaust but man survived and lives on; and the best proof of this assertion is the perpetuation of meaningful human relationships, like his with Eliezer. The artist tries to convince his friend that men must do whatever they can to alleviate human suffering; further, as a Jew he is especially obliged to do so.[54] Such a commitment, Gyula believes, takes one away from self-involved concerns and turns him toward others; indeed, to be human is to *respond* to another human being. In this perspective, Eliezer's will to die is a negation, a denial, of such response. The would-be suicide has given up, rejected the possibilities for both individual growth and human relationship; whereas the man who has chosen life keeps "moving, searching, weighing, holding out his hand, offering himself, inventing himself."

To dramatize his point of view, Gyula, on completing a portrait of his friend, burns it in the hospital room. The gesture is obviously intended to be symbolic: the face of the man in the portrait reflects a vast suffering, and the painter wants Eliezer to exorcise that part of himself which is haunted by the past. But though the portrait has been burned, the ashes remain, and so the third novel ends on the same dark chord as the first two—the anguish of a survivor who remains a corpselike, poisoned messenger from the dead.

And yet even though Eliezer continues to be imprisoned within the dark night of the soul, as a consequence of the accident and his ten weeks' stay in the hospital, he finally learns that suicide is a "false gate." In rejecting his previous notion that suicide is a courageous and necessary act in a cruelly absurd and meaningless post-Auschwitz world, he has peeled off another illusion. This does not mean, however, that he is ready to approach the right gate, the one which, as cabbalistic legend has it, leads into the orchard of truth. On the contrary, the road directly ahead will lead him to still another false gate—this one marked madness. That cycle is covered by the fourth novel, *The Town Beyond the Wall,* to which we will now turn.

"I HAVE A PLAN—TO GO MAD." Dostoevsky—this is the epigraph of *The Town Beyond the Wall.* And it is the protagonist's attraction to and ultimate rejection of madness as a possible means to the right gate which helps inform the book with an intense dialectical rhythm. At the outset of the story, as though looking to Dostoevsky's highly disturbed characters in *The Possessed,* Michael, the protagonist, wonders whether by abandoning himself to madness he actually would be revolting against his burdensome role as a poisoned messenger. Madness might blot out his need to ask questions of the Holocaust; it might allow him to be numb in heart and mind. In any event, the possibility of madness as a deliverance from shame and guilt attracts Michael, just as Eliezer of *The Accident* was drawn to the possibility of suicide as a way out of his suffering.

But is madness really the way to *the* gate? Michael begins to question as the novel unfolds. Would it really liberate him from his agony? Supposing that it led to even greater torment? Then perhaps to be afflicted by madness would be a more unendurable existence than to continue assuming the burdens of the messenger. True, the latter wanders in a twilight world without much hope of redemption; but the madman experiences the torture of being chained to the wall in an inner chamber of horrors. If such were to be his circumstances, would not suicide be infinitely more desirable than madness?

But if not through madness, by what other means could one reach and enter *the* gate? This question is precisely what a large part of the book is concerned with—the testing of various alternatives to madness.

The increasing pressure on Michael to go mad comes from the merciless interrogation and torture he is subjected to by police of the postwar Iron Country town of Szersencseváros, the place of his birth and boyhood and where he has been jailed on the suspicion of being a spy. The police officials are determined to learn by what means he entered the country; for such information they promise to go easy on him. But he is no less determined not to break down under their questioning, because the information they seek would endanger the life of Pedro, his Spanish friend and an accomplice in effecting Michael's illegal crossing of the border. Still, the gestapo-type methods of interrogation and torture by these Iron Country officials are so painful that there are moments when he is tempted to let himself fall into the oblivion of madness. He is forced to stand in a cell (ironically called "the temple"), facing a wall. The intent here is to keep him on his feet eight hours at a stretch, day and night, without food or drink, until he is ready to give the police the information they want. He is not permitted to move, to take even a step, to cross his legs or lean against the wall. It is an ordeal calculated to break even the most hardened prisoner within twenty-four hours, but Michael endures the pain, stalling for time so that Pedro can get out of the country safely.

His torture at the wall needs to be seen in other than merely literal terms. The wall is not only a wall in a jail but, symbolically, the dead-end anguish of European Jewry during the Hitler years. It may also represent the sum total of the satanic means —the gas chambers, burning ditches, gas wagons, deadly serums, machine-gun mass executions—used to destroy the bodies of

Jews. And Michael's refusal to be broken at the wall is emblematic of those European Jews who, as the narrator remarks, "more than others, possess the secret of survival, the key to the mystery of time, the formula of endurance." [55]

Neither are the attempts of the Iron Country police to make Michael talk meaningful only at the literal level. The interrogation is not simply imposed on him from the outside, it is also self-imposed; that is, the interrogation may be seen as a metaphor for Michael's unrelenting, painful inner probing regarding the Holocaust. He poses unanswerable questions concerning God, man, meaning, evil, suffering, expiation; and the disquieting force of these questions often threatens his tenuous grip on sanity.

In the end, what largely helps Michael to resist the approach of madness is his recollection of Pedro's belief that just as each man has the power to sentence himself to an internal prison of his own making, so, too, he has the capacity and will to free himself from it. Pedro, whose characteristic vibrant *élan* and tenacious will to survive remind the reader of similar qualities in Gyula of *The Accident,* would opt to pit himself against the forces of fate. Free yourself! he would have said to Michael. Yes, but how, by what means? the latter wonders, helplessly, underscoring the question that is the basis for the unifying principle of the book—a testing of various alternatives to suicide.

What alternatives? For one, silence—that is, emotional withdrawal from others. The vast silence of the survivor who does not wish to be judged for having survived by those who were not "there." Who has nothing to "explain" how it was in the camps. Through silence he can best define himself in relation to the past. But the trouble is that the living feel anxious and threatened in the presence of his silence; and they regard it as a form of hostility against them. Then, too, a sensitive man like Michael cannot remain indefinitely silent, emotionally detached from others; he is all too aware of their loneliness and inner needs. And so ultimately it is necessary that he respond in language and gesture and deed to the suffering of men. Silence is sometimes provisionally necessary for the Wieselean protagonists if they are to hear within themselves the "right" questions concerning the Holocaust past, but in the long run the desideratum for a man is, as Gyula said in *The Accident*, to hold out a hand to others.

Another alternative: Michael attempts to confront those who were indifferent to the fate of the Jewish people during the Nazi occupation of East European countries. Representative of these indifferent ones was the spectator in the window of a house adjoining the old synagogue of Szersencseváros. This spectator, a middle-aged man, sat there with a bland, unperturbed expression day after day as Jews were hunted down in the streets, beaten, and dragged off to the deportation center. Years after the war, Michael remembered—could not forget—that face as it had appeared in looking down at his parents and himself with their packs on their backs.

> A face in the window across the way. The curtains hid the rest of him; only his head was visible. It was like a balloon. Bald, flat nose, wide empty eyes. A bland face, banal, bored: no passion ruffled it. I watched it for a long time. It was gazing out, reflecting no pity, no pleasure, no shock, not even anger or interest. Impassive, cold, impersonal. The face was indifferent to the spectacle. What? Men are going to die? That's not my fault, is it now? I didn't make the decision. The face is neither Jewish nor anti-Jewish; a simple spectator, that's what it is. (P. 150.)

A "simple spectator" in the sense that he is a symbolic embodiment of the "average man" in World War II who, by his passivity and moral indifference to the suffering and murder of the oppressed, was guilty of complicity with the murderers. At the time of the deportation, Michael could not understand how this man could sit at his window looking down at the processions of human agony as though he were merely watching a theatrical performance or a pageant. Did he not *feel* anything? The murderers and the victims Michael could understand; the connections between them had their own kind of logic, twisted though it might be. But the nature of this spectator eluded his comprehension.

To confront the spectator and perhaps take revenge upon him, Michael leaves his residence in Paris and returns to Szersencseváros. Rather than continue feeling guilt and shame for having survived, he would hate and judge the spectator. Which is to say, he wants no longer to countenance himself as victim. But on coming into the presence of the spectator with his bland, bored face, Michael immediately discovers that he is unable to hate him; contempt alone is what he feels for the other. The spectator, then, is unworthy of hatred, which ought to be reserved for sentient human beings and not one who may be likened to "a stone in the street, the cadaver of an animal, a pile of dead wood." Further, Michael's inability to hate the spectator largely stems from his own characteristic aversion to being "judged" by the living for having survived; and partly from the complicated bonds connecting the executioner, victim, and spectator. True, the executioner is far more guilty than the spectator, but, nevertheless, there is, in Michael's ken, a mysterious triad linking all three roles. "Down deep," he thinks, "man is not only an executioner, not only a victim, not only a spectator: he is all three at once." And there is a further complication: in observing the spectator, in trying to understand him, Michael himself risks becoming a spectator. As he puts it: "Who observes the spectator becomes one. In his turn, he will question me. And which of our two lives will weigh heavier in the balance?"

So in the end Michael is unable to hate or judge or even humiliate the spectator. Ironically, the price of this failure is, literally, imprisonment. After Michael leaves the spectator, the latter informs on him, and he is arrested. Hence years after having been liberated from a concentration camp, he again is a prisoner. Thus it may be adduced that Michael's need to return to his hometown stemmed not only from an impulse to confront the spectator but also to satisfy an involuntary inclination to self-victimization. It is as though he must *sacrificially* become a prisoner again in order to placate a sense of guilt for having survived the Holocaust.

Since the alternatives of silence and confrontation of the

spectator have not worked, Michael, undergoing the torture of a brutal, relentless interrogation in the local jail, is driven to the point of succumbing to insanity, to a madness "in which anything is permitted, anything is possible."

It is at this critical point in Michael's circumstances that his friendship with Pedro helps to save him from a breakdown. Now he grasps more clearly than ever before the significant differences between his life-style and Pedro's. He looks for a gate that will lead to redemption; and he would like to believe that the universe is inherently founded on order and spiritual laws. By contrast, Pedro has the flexibility to believe that one can find good in evil, that God is both evil and absolution, and that man must have the courage to both listen to and oppose the word of God. Pedro has learned to live with lucidity and grace in the face of ontological uncertainties and ambiguities; and he has come to be grateful for modest expectations and simple pleasures. Unlike Michael, whose impulse is to ascertain the *meaning* of events, it is enough for Pedro to enjoy the concrete, existential immediacy of human existence.

An image of his friend, in the most excruciating moments of his torture, appears before Michael when he resolves not to break down, not to give way to insanity, during the police interrogation. Pedro would have counseled him that madness is no solution; to willingly abandon oneself to madness is to abandon one's humanity. Within the confinement of his cell, Michael imagines the voice of Pedro saying to him: "To see liberty only in madness is wrong: liberation, yes: liberty, no." What is important, then, is to remain human in the face of injustice and cruelty. And yet Michael's resources for holding on are increasingly strained to the breaking point. There are moments when he feels he is "at the end of the line," that he will soon go mad, that he cannot go on alone, that to "stay sane I've got to have someone across from me." He needs to be in a meaningful relationship with another human being.

That someone now appears and Michael is given an opportunity to protect his own sanity and to test the validity of Pedro's teaching by restoring the sanity of his cellmate, a deaf-mute

boy. At first, the latter, who had plunged into a psychotic breakdown as a result of brutal treatment by the guards, seems inac-
cessible to Michael's persistent efforts. But finally the boy begins
groping his way back to sanity. Michael's achievement therein
supports Pedro's belief that men have the freedom to protest
against human suffering by alleviating it. Such commitment,
Pedro contends, as does Gyula of *The Accident,* pulls a man
away from his own self-involved concerns and directs him
toward other human beings.

> If you could have seen yourself, framed in the doorway
> [Pedro once said to Michael], you would have believed in
> the richness of existence—as I do—in the possibility of
> having it and sharing it. It's so simple! You see a musician
> in the street; you give him a thousand francs instead of
> ten; he'll believe in God. You see a woman weeping;
> smile at her tenderly, even if you don't know her; she'll
> believe in you. You see a forsaken old man; open your
> heart to him, and he'll believe in himself. You will have
> surprised them. Thanks to you, they will have trembled,
> and everything around them will vibrate. Blessed is he
> capable of surprising and being surprised. (P. 124.)

Indeed, of all the words that Pedro had ever spoken to him and
which were to be of crucial importance in his relationship with
the deaf-mute boy, Michael recollects these:

> To say "I suffer, therefore I am" is to become the enemy
> of man. What you must say is "I suffer, therefore you are."
> Camus wrote somewhere that to protest against a universe
> of unhappiness you had to create happiness. That's an
> arrow pointing the way: it leads to another human being.
> And not via absurdity. (P. 118.)

So that finally he cannot stand by indifferently while the boy
suffers; he feels obliged to help him. This act is in keeping with
Michael's resolve to pit himself against those forces which
diminish the humanity of men. In helping the other to regain his
sanity, Michael's own progression toward madness is checked,
and his essential faith in the value of human relationship is
shored up. As the book ends, Michael is saying to the boy:

"What I say to you, pass on to you, little one, I learned from a friend—the only one I had. He's dead, or in prison. He taught me the art and necessity of clinging to humanity, never deserting humanity. The man who tries to be an angel only succeeds in making faces.

"It's in humanity itself that we find our question and the strength to keep it within limits—or on the contrary to make it universal. To flee to a sort of Nirvana—whether through a considered indifference or through a sick apathy —is to oppose humanity in the most absurd, useless, and comfortable manner possible. A man is a man only when he is among men." (P. 177.)

It's harder to remain human than to try to leap beyond humanity—this is the gist of what Michael learns from his experience as a prisoner in Szersencseváros. Taking one's life or submitting to the oblivion of insanity is no answer to the difficulties of remaining human. Instead, one needs to pit oneself against those forces which diminish a man and to continue asking questions of God and man. Perhaps in consequence of these recognitions, for the first time in a Wiesel novel, the ending contains a ray of light. Unlike *Dawn* and *Night,* which end at night and with images of the protagonist's corpselike face, *The Town Beyond the Wall* ends shortly before the approach of daybreak: "Before him [Michael] the night was receding, as on a mountain before dawn." By extension, one can speculate that some of the night, the suffering, in the protagonist is, if many years after the Holocaust, first beginning to recede.

But if now Michael willingly had accepted the moral obligation to help others, he had not yet found *the* gate. His successor, Gregor, the protagonist of *The Gates of the Forest,* will look for it in a cave within a forest of World War II Hungary, an obscure Roumanian village, in the company of some partisan fighters and finally in a synagogue of postwar Brooklyn.

The Gates of the Forest tests both the limits of disengagement and suffering and the possibilities of fervor. Also, the book dramatizes the protagonist's conflict between yearning for

an idyllic, simplified existence and accepting the hard uncertainties and complexities of his actual circumstances. There is
still another way in which to describe the central dialectic of
the novel: alternately, the protagonist views the world as benign
and then as a hostile, malevolent place; or as the narrator of
the novel describes Gregor's conflict: "A life-and-death struggle
between two angels, the angel of love and the angel of wrath,
the angel of promise and the angel of evil." The purpose of
what follows is to trace the line of this struggle and to consider its implications.

The Gates of the Forest begins in a cave located within a
forest of Transylvania during World War II. Gregor (his real
name is Gavriel, but he has assumed a Christian name largely
as a symbolic protest against the persecution he suffered as a
Jew) has managed to escape the tragic fate of the Jewish community where he had lived. Now he is hiding from the enemy
in a forest, one that is emblematic of the purity and unity of
creation that existed before the "liberation of the word," the
noisome coming of so-called civilized man. The deep silence of
the forest coincides with his own need for silence; after his
suffering as a Jew during the Nazi occupation, he prefers to be
disengaged, disassociated, from the "great, haunted cemeteries"
of Europe. In the cities beyond the forest he would feel anxious
and dispersed among men who no longer have eyes and ears
for one another. In Gregor's words:

> The forest meditates; it listens to voices instead of stifling
> them. The forest has ears, a heart, and a soul. In the forest
> simplicity is possible; simplicity belongs there. And unity,
> too. There liberty isn't forced on you like a straitjacket. I
> am what I choose to be; I am in my choice, in my will to
> choose. There is no divorce between self and its image,
> between being and acting. I am the act, the image, one and
> indivisible. Outside, things are too complicated; too many
> roads are open, too many voices call and your own is so
> easily lost. The self crumbles. (P. 221.)

The question that Wiesel poses early in the book is this:

Is the forest, as symbolic of a solitary, simplified existence and a withdrawal from other men, a justified escape for a survivor like Gregor? Isn't such isolation a way, as Pedro said to Michael in *The Town Beyond the Wall,* of leaping beyond one's humanity? Isn't it much more difficult to leave the forest and be a man among men in the town, with all its uncertain, complex, and ambiguous weathers? Unmistakably, Wiesel implies that the gates of the forest should ultimately lead back to the gates of the town. Still, the pivotal questions remain: *How* is this change to come about? *Who* is to provide the impetus for it?

Both questions are answered by the coming of the stranger into Gregor's life, a nameless fellow Jew, who has also fled from the Germans and their lackeys, the Hungarians. Gregor invites the other to share the cave with him. The stranger accepts, and at the outset his manner confuses and disturbs Gregor. There are moments when he wonders whether the other is a madman, and at other times whether he is a "messenger" from the dead. For the stranger presents an incredulous report on the destruction of entire Jewish communities, on their deportation to extermination camps, and not, as Gregor had previously supposed, to factories and labor camps. Moreover, what further disturbs Gregor is that the stranger's relationship to him is inconsistent. At first, he seems to be only a dispassionate "messenger," and then shortly he offers himself as a teacher—or perhaps Gregor has unconsciously willed the other to assume this role.

The stranger's teaching is not unlike that of two other "teachers" in Wiesel's novels, Gyula and Pedro. He contends that Gregor's kind of silence (his withdrawal from the world of men) will not do. True, Gregor has suffered, has lost his family and friends, but suffering in silence will help no one. What is wanted is not tears, not quiet suffering, but rather an active defiance of injustice and despair. One does not feel quite so helpless and despairing when, for example, one can fight off one's sorrow with laughter. Laughter for survivors

can be salutary, like the smile of Camus's Sisyphus, who persists at his endless burden of pushing and retrieving the stone.
Further, the stranger propagates the view that man must rely
solely upon himself for redemption rather than await grace from
some outside force, for instance, the coming of the Messiah.

Here the stranger's teaching coincides with that of Gregor's
father, who used to say: "The Messiah is that which makes
man more human, which takes the element of pride out of
generosity, which stretches his soul toward others." Let men be
their own Messiahs, urges the stranger. Instead of waiting for
redemption in some improbable Messianic future, let men help
one another now, in the present. And the most meaningful and
efficacious way they can do this is through the grace of friendship:

> "It is to a friend [the stranger says to Gregor] that you
> communicate. . . . Is the soul immortal, and if so why
> are we afraid to die? If God exists, how can we lay claim
> to freedom, since He is its beginning and its end? What
> is death, when you come down to it? The closing of a
> parenthesis, and nothing more? And what about life? In
> the mouth of a philosopher, these questions may have a
> false ring, but asked during adolescence or friendship,
> they have the power to change being: a look burns and
> ordinary gestures tend to transcend themselves." (P. 27.)

In appreciation for the stranger's teaching, Gregor bestows the
gift of his real name, Gavriel (which, translated from Hebrew,
means Man of God), on his nameless companion.

Seen as a whole, the function of this sequence in the cave
is clear. The protagonist recognizes the limits of a disengaged,
insulated way of life and the dangers of chronic inertia and
melancholy. Then, too, the influence of the stranger prepares
the protagonist for what presently will be his departure from the
forest and reentry into the world of men. One may speculate
that if the stranger had not appeared, Gregor would have continued to remain in a state of inertia. But when the stranger
offers his life (that is, allows himself to be captured by Hungarian soldiers) so that Gregor may be spared, the latter

recognizes that the time has come for him to leave the forest. And in the course of his subsequent adventures, Gregor was to have sufficient opportunities for testing the validity of the stranger's teachings.

Shortly after the other's departure, Gregor leaves the cave. It is important to note that he continues to bear the non-Jewish name of Gregor, for he plans to make his way in the places beyond the forest as an incognito Jew.

After leaving the forest, Gregor finds a refuge in the home of a former servant of his family, Maria, who lives in a Roumanian village. Now, although the setting has changed from a cave to that of a rural village, he is still a prisoner in the sense that Jonah was still confined when his location was changed from the hold of a ship to the belly of a whale; in both locations, Jonah was alienated from other men. Maria passes him off as her deaf-mute nephew, so that he will not need to speak and by a faulty Roumanian accent raise the suspicion of the villagers.

It is not easy to maintain an unbroken silence for many hours each day but Gregor, given his solitary existence in the forest, has already served an apprenticeship for this ordeal. Further, his public identity as a deaf-mute is not out of keeping with his inclination to feel guilty for having survived. Because he looks on himself in this way, it is not surprising that the villagers view him in a similar light. That largely is why he is forced to play the unenviable role of a silent Judas Iscariot in the village's annually produced school play.

It is at this point that Gregor breaks his silence. During the course of the play, when he is nearly beaten to death by an audience whose intense anti-Semitic animus comes violently, irrationally, to the surface, Gregor suddenly begins speaking to the villagers in the presumed voice of Judas, saying that they need to see *him* as the victim and not Christ. The symbolic point here is unmistakable: it is the Jew murdered 6,000,000 times who was crucified, and it is of him so sacrificed that the world ought to seek forgiveness.

Escaping from the villagers bent on killing him, Gregor

flees to the forest and joins a band of Jewish partisans who are
fighting the Germans. This development signals a new turning
in the book and in Gregor's changing roles. In the cave he was
the Jew in hiding; in Maria's village he was the disguised Jew,
and now, in the forest, he is transformed into the fighter. The
heroic, admirable leader of this partisan band is a childhood
friend of Gregor's, Leib the Lion, who is in the tradition of
Jewish fighter stretching from Joshua, Judas Maccabaeus, and
Bar-Cochba to the Israeli armies in the War of Independence
and the Six-Day War.

But if Gregor holds Leib in reverence, he unwittingly causes
his friend's death. The partisans had assumed that the Jews of
their respective communities had been sent to labor camps in
the East and would return after the war. When Gregor tells
them about what previously he had heard from the stranger
concerning the existence of death camps, the partisans are disbelieving. Gregor persuades them that if they wish to question
a witness to confirm this incredulous report, the stranger needs
to be rescued from the jail to which he was brought following
his capture by Hungarian soldiers. It is while involved in the res-
cue operation of the stranger that Leib is captured and killed.
Gregor feels he is guilty of having caused his friend's death;
and he openly accuses himself: "I am responsible. He who is
not among the victims is with the executioners. This was the
meaning of the holocaust: it implicated not only Abraham or
his son, but their God as well." This self-accusation is an extension of what both Gregor and earlier Wieselean survivor-
protagonists believe—"To live is to betray the dead . . . ."

His readiness to blame himself for Leib's death is denounced
by a fellow partisan, Yehuda, as an inhuman gesture. The latter
suggests that Gregor's attachment to guilt and self-incrimination
is a revealing indication of both his need to alienate himself
from others and to indulge, uselessly, in further suffering. "You
insist upon suffering alone. Such suffering shrinks you, diminishes you." Yehuda then goes on to argue that such self-lacera-
tion is hardly a means to a true liberation of the spirit. Instead,

what is wanted are human beings constructing bridges to one another, even in the face of the awesome Void. "You say, 'I'm alone.' Someone answers, 'I'm alone too.' There's a shift in the scale of power. A bridge is thrown between the two abysses."

Ideally, then, suffering ought to make us more open, more accessible to others, rather than the reverse; and precisely because human existence is full of so much pain and unhappiness, it is important to give one's best response to the demands of love and friendship. In short, Yehuda speaks to Gregor in the same key that Gyula did to Eliezer and Pedro to Michael. True, earlier the stranger had similarly spoken to Gregor about the meaning of friendship, but the latter had not really been ready then to hear the message.

After the war, Gregor and his wife, Clara, formerly a partisan and Leib's mistress, immigrate to the United States, and they settle in a Brooklyn community. It is essentially a marriage of love, and yet Gregor does not feel he is any closer to the gate he has been searching for; redemption seems as far off as before; he is still in bondage to the griefs of the past, and his day-to-day existence in the realms of normalcy is flat, joyless, routinized.

In a period of severe depression, Gregor makes a pilgrimage-like visit to a Hasidic synagogue in Williamsburg. The worshipers that he enviously observes there are so open and happy that they seem to flow out of themselves with spontaneous singing and dancing. They have no need to wait for the Messiah; a thousand times a day they bring him down to earth with their joyous immersion in the present, in the moment. In their fervor, they body forth the possibilities of a life-style that heretofore, given the tragedy of the Holocaust, Gregor had considered inappropriate.

But how does one attain fervor? he wonders. The Hasidic rabbi of the synagogue, whose followers look up to him as a zaddik, a man of wisdom and saintliness, responds to Gregor's question during the latter's visit. Get out of the solitary self, the rabbi urges; cease being in love with suffering; become one, joyously and in trust, with others.

> At intervals he [the rabbi] pounded the table with his fist. Ferocious and irresistible, he demanded greater enthusiasm and abandon. Don't caress your soul as if it were a body, feeding on kisses. Beat it without humiliating it; whip it without diminishing it; drive it out of your self in order that it may rejoin its source and become one with it in the *Heichal Hanegina,* the sanctuary of melody—it's there I await you in a secret promise. (P. 193.)

But Gregor is not to be easily convinced; he is full of anger and bitterness. "How can anyone believe in God after what has happened?" he challenges the rabbi. And so the argument between them is joined and rages until finally Gregor forces the other to make the admission that God, like man, is often guilty of injustice and cruelty. Still, the rabbi contends, one can defy Him as much by singing and dancing as by shouts of protest or chronic melancholy or suffering or silence.

> "Do you know what the song hides? A dagger, an outcry. Appearances have a depth of their own which has nothing to do with the depth. When you come to our celebrations you'll see how we dance and sing and rejoice. There is joy as well as fury in the hasid's dancing. It's his way of proclaiming. 'You don't want me to dance; too bad, I'll dance anyhow. You've taken away every reason for singing, but I shall sing. I shall sing of the deceit that walks by day and the truth that walks by night, yes, and of the silence of dusk as well. You didn't expect my joy, but here it is; yes, my joy will rise up; it will submerge you.' " (P. 198.)[56]

What is the meaning of human suffering? Gregor further interrogates the rabbi. For if there is no meaning, then God is indeed either dead or malevolent. The rabbi replies that suffering is God's way of testing man.

> For suffering contains the secret of creation and its dimension of eternity; it can be pierced only from the inside.

Suffering betters some people and transfigures others. At the end of suffering, of mystery, God awaits us. (P. 201.)

Suffering as a meaningful trial—was this the gate, Gregor wonders, that he had been searching for? And was the God of justice and redemption waiting behind that gate? With the emergence of these questions, the movement of all five novels has come full turn. The archetypal Wieselean protagonist has journeyed a long way from the embittered young man of *Night* who categorically viewed the suffering of victims and survivors as cruelly meaningless.

Thus Gregor's meeting with the rabbi marks another *tikkun,* a turning, in his search for the gate of redemption. This development occurs when, as part of a minyan, he recites Kaddish in a Hasidic synagogue. A Yeshiva boy invites and leads him to this minyan; which is to say, symbolically, that the child within the adult directs the latter back to the source of his childhood faith in God. Gregor's return is not only symbolic; it is *actually* to a familiar place of his boyhood, a synagogue; and significantly, the synagogue is also the setting for the opening pages of the first novel.

Here it is instructive to recall the central settings of the preceding novels. The concentration camp in the middle and ending sections of *Night* is followed by the secret headquarters and cellar execution chamber of the terrorist fighters in *Dawn.* *The Accident* takes place in a hospital. Much of *The Town Beyond the Wall* occurs in a jail. These changing central locations in the first four novels are as so many signposts for charting the stages of the Wieselean hero's journey. He survives the camps and is liberated. But in going underground with the terrorist movement, he is again immolated, this time in an inner prison of self-hate for becoming the executioner. In *The Accident,* at the bottom of his despair, he invites an accident, as though to precipitate and confront the decision of whether to choose life or death. Following his convalescence in the hospital, he undergoes imprisonment in the town beyond the wall. But though behind bars there, he is not the passive, sacrificial

victim of Auschwitz and Buchenwald; rather, he opts to actively help his brothers-in-suffering.

Seen in this perspective of place as symbol, the synagogue
scene ending *The Gates of the Forest* is telling. For the movement from the synagogue of Eliezer's boyhood in *Night* to the
Hasidic synagogue in the last novel suggests that the hero has
begun to come full circle in his journey, one marked by the
following high points: as a boy, witnessing the mass burning
of children, he lost faith in God; as a young man in Palestine
he sought to exorcise the Holocaust past by becoming an executioner; as a survivor in New York he attempted suicide
to escape from the burden of guilt and suffering; as a prisoner
in the town beyond the wall, he discovered the importance of
responding to others; and in postwar Brooklyn he was attracted
to the possibilities of faith and fervor as a life-style.

During his visit to the Brooklyn synagogue, he finds himself
desiring a single identity as a man and Jew. This inclination is
signaled in the book's ending by his abandonment of the name
Gregor and the reclamation of his real name, Gavriel, an act
which indicates that he is ready to *choose* himself as a Jew. In
coming to the Hasidic synagogue to recite Kaddish, to pray to
God for the souls of his father and Leib, and for "the soul of
his childhood," the Wieselean hero returns, if only provisionally,
to his boyhood faith, which had been consumed in the flames of
Auschwitz. And now, four books later, the older protagonist,
Gavriel, reciting Kaddish, proclaims that "great and terrible is
the God of the Jews, that his ways are righteous and impene-
trable, that he has the right to hide himself, to change face and
sides, that he who gives life and light may also take them away."
The recitation of this prayer suggests that the cry of Job has
become his own. God has remained silent while millions were
destroyed during the Holocaust and yet Gavriel, the Jobian
survivor, chooses to speak to him—and to wait for a response.

But the only voice he hears is one within himself urging
him to love God, saying: "It's not a question of him but of
yourself. Your love, rather than his, can save you." It is as

though this voice were saying: Stop feeling guilty for having survived. It is not necessary that you pray to God for forgiveness; rather, "forgive" yourself for having survived, bury the dead, choose life, and try to live with fervor.

But there must be struggle, Gavriel realizes; redemption will not simply happen to us by itself and from without. This struggle ought to take place not in cloistered, solitary places of the forest but rather in the streets and houses of the town; that is, one ought not to take easy refuge in a disassociated, hermetic existence; instead, one needs to confront the uncertainties and problems of life in the modern world. This means, among other things, looking with steadiness and compassion at the "thousand faces" of all men: faces of ugliness, hatred, bitterness, torment, chaos, and also those of peacefulness, desire, love.

What is the novel's "last word"? In reciting the Kaddish, Gavriel reserves his final prayer for the soul of his dead friend, Leib.

> The last *Kaddish* would be for him, to ask that the warrior find peace; that the angels, jealous of his strength and, above all, of his purity, cease to persecute him, that he himself cease to cause suffering to those who once loved him and still love him. Yes, the last *Kaddish* would be for him, our messenger to heaven. (P. 226.)

This last moment of the book, then, charts the distance the Wieselean hero has traveled since the time of the first three novels. *Night* ends with the image of Eliezer's corpselike face and *Dawn* concludes with the image of Elisha's tormented reflection in a window facing a dawn of "greyish light the color of stagnant water." *The Accident* ends with an image of ashes— the remains of Eliezer's portrait. By contrast, heaven is the final image in *The Gates of the Forest;* Gavriel prays for the soul of Leib, "our messenger to heaven." What I believe Wiesel, consciously or otherwise, is saying here is that he prays for peace, an end to the suffering of his survivor-protagonist, Eliezer-Elisha-Michael-Gavriel.

Let us now sum up the protagonist's journey through the first five novels. At the foot of the road was the town of his birth and boyhood in Hungary—the innocent days. Then the Germans came: came the long journey in sealed freight cars to "labor camps" in the East, came the crematoria fires, children burning in mass graves and dying on gallows. All through this nightmare of history, the protagonist kept asking the same question: Why does God permit the suffering to go this way? Why doesn't he show mercy to the oppressed? But there was no answer, only a vast silence. And in the vacuum of that awful silence, the protagonist finally turned to accuse Him. His faith had been consumed in the flames of Auschwitz but the anger and bitterness of his accusation against God helped steel him for living through the Holocaust.

He survived and returned from the realm of the dead to the living. And therein is the harsh irony—that instead of continuing to accuse God and man for what had happened, he turned to accusing himself for having survived; he who had been one of the Nazis' victims now took upon himself a burden of guilt and shame. It is as though he said to himself: I am alive, so therefore I am guilty; for no one having experienced on his flesh the horrors of absolute evil and oppression should want to go on living in such an impure world. And though continuing to live, he did so, in his own eyes, as a poisoned messenger. He felt that the very sight of his presence disturbed others, incriminated their "innocence." He had survived the camps, survived an attempt at suicide in New York, and now he was spent, empty, adrift without direction.

Because he could not grasp the incomprehensible, what had been during that season in hell, because he could not explain it to himself, not alone others, he fell into a depressed silence. He had tried, unsuccessfully, to hate the executioners and their accomplices. His attempt at suicide had failed. Language, mere words, did not enable him to speak meaningfully to the living, to those who were not "there." So he was left with the role of the silent, poisoned messenger, despised in his own eyes and disturbing in the eyes of the innocent.

And this towering burden of guilt and shame would have been borne, without diminishment, to the end of his days. But finally a light was born in the darkness, and he saw himself as a brand miraculously plucked from the fire; he *had* endured. Perhaps there was meaning in this singular and astonishing fact.

Then he began to look back with increasing clarity and steadiness at the nightmarish days of the Holocaust. And he saw that not only had there been the victims but also those valiant men who had pitted their pride and dignity against the inhuman. Beside the images of oppression and death he could place the memories of friends—Gyula, Pedro, Leib. The Nazis had been, murder and genocide had been, but so had friendship. Men brought suffering and death to other men, but sometimes they brought the gift and grace of friendship.

Until that point in his journey, haunted by the ghosts of the past, the Wieselean hero had been looking back. And now he came to consider the possibilities of living with fervor in the *present*. In meeting the Hasidic rabbi and his followers, it was as though he were asking them, "Teach me fervor." He had known suffering and death, the loss of faith in God and man, and now he wanted to know a joy akin to their dancing and singing. He had undergone the transmutations of victim, executioner, would-be suicidist, would-be madman, and solitary, and now he wanted peace, rest.

Still, the questioning had not ended, would perhaps never end; the Wieselean hero would go on posing unanswerable questions concerning God, man, and the Holocaust. Unanswerable in the sense that Michael meant when he said to the deaf-mute boy: "The essence of man is to be a question, and the essence of the question is to be without answer . . . . The depth, the meaning, the very salt of man is his constant desire to ask the question ever deeper within himself, to feel even more intimately the existence of an unknowable answer." So the questioning would go on, would not let him rest, but neither had the singing of the Jew ended. And as long as the singing and the questioning went on, the Eternal People would con-

tinue resisting and contending and enduring against the Angel
of Death.

The struggle to survive [Gavriel plans to say to his wife]
will begin here, in this room, where we are sitting. Whether
or not the Messiah comes doesn't matter; we'll manage
without him. It is because it is too late that we are commanded to hope. We shall be honest and humble and
strong, and then he will come, he will come every day,
thousands of times every day. He will have no face, because he will have a thousand faces. The Messiah isn't
one man, Clara, he's all men. As long as there are men
there will be a Messiah. One day you'll sing, and he will
sing in you. (P. 225.)

5

Spiritual Resistance

A literature of blood and ashes, unbearably painful to read. A boy on a gallows in a concentration camp courtyard, and underneath the dangling corpse one of the prisoners standing at enforced attention thinks: "Where is God? There he is— hanging on the gallows" (*Night*). A Nazi official, with immense satisfaction, watches a film showing scenes of Jews being herded into cattle cars for shipment to the "East" (*The Stronghold*). A German gouges a child's eyes with a penknife (*Blood from the Sky*). Captured Russian officers are led to a shower, given a bar of soap, then shot by an SS man through a hole in a wall (*The Long Voyage*). Squashed babies are carried out by the legs, like chickens, from a deportation cattle car ("This Way for the Gas"). A young prisoner in Auschwitz is unable to shed a single tear on learning that his sister has been sexually abused by Nazis (*House of Dolls*). A Jewish child is taken by his German "protector" to a remote place in the mountains and left there to die (*Soul of Wood*).

But such dark moments in Holocaust literature do not tell the whole story; there is also that body of writing which may be termed the literature of spiritual resistance. It often portrays situations wherein characters actively contend against those conditions in the ghettos and concentration camps which diminish the humanity of men. Though often broken in body, they refuse to be broken in spirit. What sustains this resolve?

Not necessarily religious belief; indeed, many of these characters proclaim that following Auschwitz, "God is dead." But they have other reasons for contending against the forces of darkness. Sometimes they strive to alleviate the agony of their comrades-in-suffering. In some instances, Jewish characters exercise resistance out of a granite commitment to share the tragic fate of other Jews. Or they resist sheerly out of an obdurate pride to withstand being broken, to deprive their Nazi jailors of yet another victory. In any event, works containing the theme of spiritual resistance have this in common: they are not nihilistic in tone or perspective; they are not unduly concerned with literary manipulation and embellishment; they do not portray the atrocities in order to shock the reader.

But this is to state what spiritual resistance literature is not. Defined positively, such works are usually characterized by the authors' directness of narrative method, the intense concern of Jewish characters for the common welfare and destiny of other Jews, and the iron determination of the protagonists to maintain pride and dignity despite the attempts of their Nazi persecutors to dehumanize them. If I had only one sentence in which to sum up the key characteristic of such works, I would say that it is the extraordinary efforts of persecuted people to be immensely human in the face of unspeakably brutalizing circumstances.

Within the framework of the above-stated characteristics, one would have to rule out as spiritual resistance literature some highly acclaimed short stories and novels. Here I have in mind such works as Ka-tzetnik's *House of Dolls,* T. Borowski's "This Way for the Gas" and "The People Who Walked," and Jakov Lind's *Landscape in Concrete.*

What works against *House of Dolls* is that it makes too many demands on our sense of pity. Undeniably, Ka-tzetnik passionately feels the tragic situations described in his novel. But the trouble is that he, perhaps unwittingly, insists too much on our response to the minutiae of the horrors experienced by his protagonists. It is as though he assumes that a cumulative, nonrestrictive cataloging of grotesque details will upset us far more than a few selective ones. Yet how long can the reader go on drawing back from the bizarre and macabre? Beyond a certain point this capacity to so respond is blunted, if not exhausted. As David Rousset has remarked: "Misery that goes too deep arouses not compassion but repugnance."

What is characteristic of Ka-tzetnik's narrative manner in this novel is the tendency of the narrator to *talk at* the reader. When, for example, the prisoner-"doctor" of the Auschwitz infirmary, Harry, is working on the swollen abscessed knee of a fellow prisoner, there is this overwrought passage:

> He lances and probes into the living flesh, as one probes with a knife point down to the core of a rotten fruit. He scrapes and gouges with the scalpel, deeper, deeper. When will he hit bottom? There's no end to it. What is there beyond the swollen rottenness? Is there no bone there at all? Where in a man is the core of life? Here, a man in the chair, his leg slung across Harry's knees. The scalpel delves deeper and deeper, and he sits there as if the legs were not his at all. Tomorrow this very leg will march him out to Baustelle! The same leg is about to carry him out of the sick bay and up into his hutch. Is this flesh alive, or not? And if not, where in a man is the core of life? (P. 91.)

But it is not merely these qualities which preclude *House of Dolls* from being considered as authentically in the literature of spiritual resistance. I refer to the inclination of its characters to suffer passively. Of determined, sustained wrestling against their afflictions and misery there is little evidence in the book, with the possible exception of the moral support the Jewish girls, Fella and Daniella (who have been forced to serve as prostitutes for the German officials and guards of the camp), give to each other. Even so, when Daniella, in an acutely distressed state of mind, runs into a forbidden zone and is shot down by a sentry, this death, coloring as it does the ultimate effect of the book, is hardly an expression of spiritual resistance.

Liberation from further misery this suicidal act is, but an act of spiritual freedom, no. Daniella had sought death because she no longer felt able to contend against her circumstances.

Jakov Lind, the author of *Soul of Wood*, a collection of short stories, and a novel, *Landscape in Concrete*, has been widely praised for his style and uses of fantasy, grotesque characters, and lunatic humor. Certainly these qualities are conspicuous throughout *Landscape in Concrete*. The protagonist, Gauthier Bachmann, a *Wehrmacht* sergeant in the last days of the Second World War, goes on a macabre odyssey in search of his regiment, from which he was separated on the Russian front. Army doctors have discharged Bachmann after finding him mentally unfit, but this ruling does not deter him from wanting to rejoin his regiment and to fight for the honor and glory of the Fatherland. The novel charts a series of adventures that befall Bachmann along the route of his search. In France, he is tricked into shooting a homosexual *Wehrmacht* cook who deserted his unit. In Navrik, Norway, on orders from a vindictive quisling, he shoots four members of a prominent local family. Returning to Germany, he is declared sane by another board of army doctors. As the story closes, Bachmann is still determined to find his regiment.

Nazi Germany was indeed a place of organized madness, which men like Wohlbrecht[57] in *Soul of Wood* and Bachmann in *Landscape in Concrete* epitomize. Lind's wit is lethal in pointing up the compulsions of Germans for order, duty, solid burgher comfort, hygienic cleanliness, fate, and "universal cosmic unity." But if the characters and their situations are true to the demented world of the Third Reich, the trouble is that the reader never gets beyond the frozen atmosphere of Lind's landscape: "As far as the eye could see a desert of ashes under a lead-gray sky. The stillness was palpable, as colorless and bare as the walls of a monk's cell. Nothing moved in the deathly silence, nothing crawled, rustled, or murmured." This same gelid condition is especially present in Lind's grotesques. They feel neither anger nor hate nor concern for one another. Mainly they keep cool. Bachmann describes how "without batting an eyelash" he killed four people: "No, I didn't lose control of myself, I wasn't upset, I kept cool. That's the main thing." [58] All this is in keeping with Lind's apparent intention to underscore the inhuman in Hitler's Germany. But the unrelieved, chilling lifelessness of the characters repels the reader.

Whatever hate for the murderous robots of Nazi Germany lies behind the writing of the story, such emotion is insulated from the reader by the icily manipulated performance of grotesque caricatures. The novel becomes a sick-joke cartoon strip on a human disaster. In the end, Lind's novel does not bring us closer to the pertinent questions concerning the Holocaust. Ultimately this writer's coolness of presentation produces a coolness of effect. Hence the third and fourth lines of the first chapter may be read as a comment upon the book's essential flaw: "A landscape without faces is like air nobody breathes. A landscape in itself is nothing."

Tadeusz Borowski's[59] short stories cannot be criticized for the kind of overwriting that flaws *House of Dolls*. If anything, he goes to the other extreme in the cold-blooded detachment with which he portrays his characters and their situations. Literary critics have especially admired the brilliantly controlled, unemotional tone of Borowski's short story "This Way for the Gas." Here the inhuman are not only the Nazis with their "shiny, brutal faces" but, unfortunately, the prisoners assigned to a work detail whose function it is to strip fellow Jews of their food, money, and valuable belongings and turn the loot over to camp officials. Despising themselves for submitting to this degrading assignment in order to save their own skins, these prisoners pathologically hate the victims they betray. Hence a member of this work detail, referring to his victims, cries out:

> I am furious, furious, unreasonably furious at these people —that I must be here because of them. I don't feel any pity

for them. I'm not sorry that they're going to the gas. Damn them all! I could throw myself at them with my fists. (P. 43.)

And in the story "The People Who Walked" the narrator, an Auschwitz prisoner, continues to play soccer while coolly observing in the near distance processions of men, women, and children moving toward the bathhouse. On seeing an old man run to join the ranks of one such procession, the narrator remarks to himself: "It seems very amusing to watch someone who was in such a hurry to get to the gas chambers." Here, too, as in "This Way for the Gas," Borowski seems more concerned with indicting the victim rather than the executioner. He eschews rendering even a semblance of the compassionate relationships among the oppressed that are numerously recorded in the literature of spiritual resistance.

Having pointed to some examples of what spiritual resistance literature is not, I turn now to some works illustrating what it is. Earlier I remarked that many of the persecuted in the camps and ghettos were able to resist the efforts of the Nazis to defile their humanity. If they could not fight back against their oppressors with guns, they resisted with their wills; they exercised an inner freedom that the worst sadists could not deprive them of. Hence Tania, the protagonist of the highly talented Zdena Berger's sensitive novel *Tell Me Another Morning,* resolves to protect her sense of identity:

> The only thing that remains is the I in me. I find suddenly some strange pleasure in knowing that when I die I will die the same, unchanged, as when I was me. It matters very much. Yes, as I was.
> Keep that last thing. Hang on to it as to the last wall. (P. 78.)

Hang on to it—to one's most particular sense of identity; he who saw no purpose in doing this was well on the way to becoming one of the walking dead. Tania's resolve became her shield and armor against the daily assaults of the nightmarish existence behind barbed wire. And it is important to note that though she was hardly oblivious to the constant harassment of prisoners, the fires and stench of the crematoria, the skeletal figures of children, she chose not to stare too long at the numbing particulars of horror and death. Mainly she looked to whatever life-giving sources were to be found in Auschwitz. So it is that on seeing birds passing overhead (a moment in flight that capsules so much of Tania's longing for freedom), she thinks: "Their narrow wings open small against the cold blue of the sky." And of some nearby flowers she observes, with telling precision of line and tone: "The begonias were turning yellow. The pink had disappeared altogether, but the blooms were consistent. The peppermoths were above the bushes."

When Miss Berger does render terrifying details of the Auschwitz inferno, her inclination is to use understatement. "How sweet they smell," says Eva to her friend Tania as the two come upon "a young girl, lying face up" on the ground. And in a calm, almost dispassionate voice, Tania thinks: "In the wide space of the outstretched legs the grass is yellow." In sum, Miss Berger never insists upon horror for its own sake. Yet the suffering of Tania and her fellow sufferers comes through with unforgettable force.

Josef Bor's *The Terezin Requiem* is not brimming with craft. The narrative is not full of surprises, intricacies, Henry Jamesian "secrets of the kitchen" techniques. The characters are neither multidimensional nor indelibly individualized. If Bor has a gift for physical description, it is not evident in this work. What then is evident? The writer's tremendous respect for his subject matter, for the extraordinary achievement of the human spirit in the face of the inhuman.

The achievement was a performance of Verdi's *Requiem* in 1944 within Theresienstadt by the brilliant conductor Raphael Schächter, musicians, and some 150 singers. That the performance came off at all was a miracle.[60] The rehearsals took place in a dim cellar; the singers and musicians were frequently deported; instruments had to be smuggled into the ghetto; the shadow of the SS stretched over the rehearsals; the musicians were emaciated, exhausted, psychologically harried. Yet for eighteen months Schächter and his company practiced on. Overcoming a multitude of obstacles—not the least of which was the inherent musical complexities of the *Requiem* itself— the musicians fashioned something beautiful, a work of art.

Verdi's work was essentially intended as a prayer to the dead, but Schächter and his colleagues produced an expression of man's irrepressible will to freedom. The music they arranged was intended to say to the Nazis who were present at the final performance: "You have marked us as the seed of Abraham, and now we, prisoners in a Jewish camp, exult before you. You have not broken us, you will not break us!" That is why the conductor shaped the *Requiem* so that instead of ending on its customary quiet note, it concluded "defiantly, like a demand, a challenge." The last *Libera me!* of the singers is a passionate affirmation of the human spirit in defiance of those who would debase it.

Thus the performance of the *Requiem* before Nazi officials was an act of spiritual resistance in the way that Janusz Korczak[61] and his children walked through the streets of Warsaw toward the *Umschlagplatz.* Or in the way that Rabbi David Shapiro[62] refused to abandon his people in the Warsaw ghetto, even though officials of the Catholic Church had offered him an asylum in another part of the city. Or in the way that Emmanuel Ringelblum and Chaim Kaplan, risking death, persisted in keeping journals out of a historical sense of responsibility to future generations.

So, too, Schächter and his colleagues were committed to the same principle of spiritual resistance, except that, instead of using prose like Ringelblum and Kaplan, they affirmed themselves through music. And when the Terezin inhabitants in the audience heard the *Requiem,* they responded with tremendous emotion. When the last note of the final rehearsal had died away there was no applause, only a stillness, and for a moment the conductor thought he had failed. What he could not know, since his back was turned to the audience, is that the listeners were so moved they could not immediately applaud. Dazed, they were looking on with "tear-filled eyes." Then, in silence, they rose to their feet and the applause finally came, "like a thunderstorm," becoming "ever more violent, and nothing could quiet it."

In keeping with the theme of spiritual resistance that, like a great burning light, irradiates the book, Schächter, following the performance's conclusion, deliberately does not bow to the Nazis in the audience. Such pride is warranted, for he has succeeded in achieving his original intention, to show up the

> mendacity of perverted ideas, of pure and impure blood, of superior and inferior races, to expose them precisely in a Jewish camp, and precisely through the medium of art, in the field where a man's true worth can best be recognized. (Pp. 7–8.)

Just as the walls of Theresienstadt are symbolically penetrated by the performance of Schächter and his musicians, so, too, the walls of the Warsaw ghetto are transcended by the Jewish populace of John Hersey's epic, *The Wall*. A half million people, crowded within a hundred blocks, ravaged by typhus, exposed to every brutalizing condition, and yet what one sees is the dignity and pride of a people. Through the omniscient eyes of the historian Noach Levinson are presented those instances wherein the populace variously exhibits inner resistance against the Nazis: Levinson's diary records vignettes of Jewish home life, synagogue worship, Jewish Self-Aid activities, secret school classes and lectures on Jewish literature (e.g., the one that was delivered in an underground bunker on the artistry of Peretz), the planting of gardens and vegetable plots in bombed-out sites, and the illegal (from the Nazis' standpoint) transference of books from the Bronislaw Grosser Library, which had been placed outside the ghetto walls.

In this latter vignette occurs the unforgettable moment when Berson, Levinson, and four comrades (all of whom are ardent readers), after four nights of digging and tunneling, recover books that are treasured by the Jewish populace. A sack of books, which the powerfully built Berson is dragging, breaks. In retrieving the scattered books out of the dirt, Berson picks them up "daintily one by one between the tips of his thumbs and forefingers, so as not to soil them, with his little fingers elevated to the teacup position." A muscular man, and yet he delicately holds a book—so much of traditional Jewish veneration for books is compacted into that image! And such veneration at a time when the Nazis wanted the Jew to remain on his knees was surely a way of standing erect before the oppressors.

André Schwarz-Bart's *The Last of the Just* preeminently speaks to the theme of spiritual resistance in Holocaust literature. But the protagonist, Ernie Levy, has to undergo several trials before he is ready to exercise such resistance. As a boy in Germany, he feels helpless before the aggressive hostility of anti-Semites; and it seems to him that the Jews of his community are also easily intimidated; their persecutors torment them with impunity, as though they are merely swatting flies. Under such circumstances, if a Jew wished to survive, it was incumbent upon him to be meek, inconspicuous; anti-Semitic insults were to be endured in silence and shame. "Let me stay tiny!" Ernie thinks. In other words, let me be so inconspicuous that the Germans will not notice me. To be "invisible"—that, too, is the intent of the Jews living in Ernie's community. In the face of persecution the only physical response that they sometimes permit themselves is to raise their hands toward the sky in an immemorial gesture of resignation and a plea for mercy. Of such Jews, Ernie thinks, bitterly: "They were pure, gentle and silly, they knew only how to weep and extend their naked hands."

The culmination of Ernie's feelings of shame and humiliation occurs when he is beaten up by some Hitler Youth hooligans.

During this incident he involuntarily lifts his hands in the very gesture that he had depreciated in others: "They fluttered in the air, up against the wheel of the sun, as if he did not know what to do with them and wished simply to testify to his own impotence."

Directly following the brutal assault upon him, Ernie has an intense need to let out his anger and hatred.[63] And so he does, on insects. He crushes, destroys scores of insects in a meadow. This act is the expression of a largely unconscious need to transform himself from the sacrificial victim to the executioner. In one of the most violent scenes in Holocaust literature, Ernie runs, like one possessed, through the meadow, his hands "gummy with vermin," trapping and crushing insects.

The insect slaughter hardly eases his inner turmoil. Ernie feels that somehow it is not only the hooligans but also himself who is not worthy as a human being. Thus, lying near the destroyed insects, he berates himself: *"I was nothing."* Here, as elsewhere through the novel, Schwarz-Bart's understanding of his characters is accurate. Having been humiliated in his own eyes, Ernie turns his anger in on himself. Next, in a state of extreme depression, he attempts to commit suicide. First he cuts his wrists and then jumps out of a third-floor window, landing in a courtyard below. Miraculously, he survives the fall, though suffering extensive bone and spinal fractures. On returning home after two years in a hospital bed, he finds the weeping and praying of pious Jews in the town's synagogue even more lamentable than before his suicide attempt. Observing them at prayer, he thinks: "My god, they're just as innocent as ever." Why must this be? he wonders. Why must the Jew, in country after country, carry misery and suffering around on his back, like a hump? For Ernie there is nothing ennobling about such suffering, and he agrees with his father's melancholy remark: *"To be a Jew is impossible."*

Nor does this point in the story constitute the nadir of Ernie's despair. Schwarz-Bart sugarcoats nothing; a hard, exacting light is focused on Ernie's step-by-step moral and psychological debilitation. In a section called "The Dog," Ernie, as a young man in France, to which he fled from Nazi Germany, takes on the disguises of a degenerate non-Jew. In so doing, he changes his name from Ernie to Ernest, alters his dress, grooming, gait, voice, and even his diet, stuffing himself with raw, bloody meats and sausages of all kinds, until he develops a "huge, fat paunch." Having broken away from his former religious faith (he could not forgive a God who had allowed his father, mother, brothers, and sisters to be imprisoned in a concentration camp) and seeing himself as a "dirty dog," he acts like one. Hence in a Marseilles restaurant, Ernie drunkenly runs round and round a table on all fours, barking wildly:

> First it was vigorous "arf-arf's" that he barked against his plateful of bones, then a spectacular tumble, after which he got up on all fours and, amid general hilarity, galloped grotesquely around the large table. One of the women threw him a bone, which he dug into, teeth flashing, in a perfect mimicry. Screams of laughter. Ecstatic women writhing. Finally he springs at Mélanie on all fours, and tries to bite off a pretty hunk of flesh. (P. 325.)

Ernie's experiment in living as a "dog" ends in failure; it is not easy for a man of his innate sensitivity to playact at being coarse and brutal. Then, too, although his external appearance and manner is disguised, in his own eyes he remains a Jew. Neither does he feel easy at remaining "free," a Jew-in-hiding, when his entire family has been taken off to concentration camps. Finally he cannot shut out the inner question immemorially asked of Jews—"Where are you?" Ernie's way of responding "Here I am!" [64] to this imperative summons is to turn himself into the Drancy concentration camp. The guards who intern him are disbelieving that a Jew who had the opportunity to save his own skin indefinitely should have voluntarily chosen imprisonment, and they suspect him of being a simpleton.

Once behind barbed wire, Ernie does not regret his act; indeed, a satisfying sense of peace comes over him, and he has "no intention of . . . separating himself from the humble procession of Jewish people." [65] Refusing to give way to despair, he attempts to assuage the pain of his crippled sweetheart, Golda, a prisoner in the women's section of the camp. And on learning that Golda's name has been placed on a deportation list, he pleads with a camp official to have his name added to the list. The official, though complying with the request, cannot understand why Ernie should willingly want to hasten his own death. Ernie's explanation is terse: "M. Blum, wherever there are Jews, there is my kingdom."

In the freight car bearing him and others to Auschwitz, Ernie comforts a group of fifteen sick and frightened children who have been separated from their parents. Seated beside corpses and upon straw "soiled by human filth," Ernie, rather than crush their frail hopes by telling them the truth, lies that it is the kingdom of Israel to which they are going, to a place where they would have plenty to eat and where *"there are no Germans or railway cars or anything that hurts."* And when one of his fellow deportees hostilely challenges his right to allay the children's fears by telling them such fairy tales, Ernie replies: "Madame . . . there is no room for truth here." [66]

When they come to the "kingdom of Israel," the platform ramp at Auschwitz, Ernie knows what is going to happen to most of the deportees; and he chooses not to be separated from Golda during the selection, even though the infamous Dr. Mengele had already certified him as physically fit enough for assignment to a work detail. Knowing that he would soon be dead, Ernie, as he and the others walk toward the "bathhouse," might have panicked. Instead, in those last few minutes of his life, while carrying a little boy who had fainted and speaking lovingly to Golda, he is composed, almost serene.

Standing in the darkness of a sealed gas chamber, concerned to shorten the agony of the children near him, Ernie has the presence of mind to cry out: "Breathe deeply, my lambs, and quickly!" And then, even as the fumes of Cyclon B gas enter his lungs, in a gesture that supremely embodies the strength and elevation of the spiritual resistance theme in Holocaust literature, he places his arm around Golda in "loving protection."

6

The Interrogators

Despite their season in hell, they are hardly broken. To survive the Holocaust and then to relive it through their writing, these survivor-writers had to be strong. How many times during the dark years had they commanded themselves to hold on to the day of liberation, so that they could tell their stories, bear witness? Surely it is in the realm of miracle that in one moment of recent history, men, starving, clad in rags, ailing and barely alive, could resolve to tell their stories someday; and then, in another moment, only a little over two decades later, these stories are in print.

But beyond this astonishing fact, what gives the presence of these survivor-writers an awesome strength is that they *accuse*. Brands plucked out of the fire, they have earned the right to be accusers. They do not come before their readers to explain or to expiate or to ask for sympathy. They do not reach for lessons where there are none. Rather they accuse man—and sometimes God—for what men did to men. They accuse the murderers and their accomplices and those who were silent when children were burning. And what is more terrible, they sometimes indict themselves for having risen phoenixlike out of the ashes, for having survived while others close to them had not. Hence the cry of a Wieselean survivor: "He who is not among the victims is with the executioners."

Through what means do they make these accusations? Mainly through interrogation—through questions that come not out of the study or the library but the flames. As such, they do not seek "balanced" computations or "precise" judgment in their writing. They write with a tremendous sense of urgency, as though for them the camps are still there. Perhaps they have no alternative: not to question, not to confront the "undigested" past, would be to self-inflict the final indignity. For if their experiences during the dark years "taught" them any one thing it is this—not to remain silent. True, the Holocaust remains in the realm of mystery, the incomprehensible (and perhaps inexpressible), but nevertheless these survivor-writers do not feel free to desist from interrogation.

They are especially concerned with two questions: First, why did many of the oppressed, despite the severest kinds of pressures, in a time when the very image of man had become defiled, struggle to hold on, *tzu iberlebyn?* And, second, in the words of Dr. Ekstein (*Night of the Mist*), on what did it depend whether a man remained a man—that is, human despite the brutalizing conditions of the camps and closed ghettos? I shall briefly summarize the nature of several writers' essential responses to these questions.

Some persisted in "holding on" not merely to save their own skin or to achieve an ultimate revenge over the enemy but, more positively, out of a reverence for life itself; by their continued existence, they sought to sanctify life. Thus, for example, in the journals of Ringelblum, Kruk, Kalmanovitch, and Kaplan, we read about a community that was able to sing, dance, attend concerts, lectures, and plays even as the enemy stood inside its gates. Altogether, it was as though they were saying to the enemy: "You hold life cheap, we do not. It is you who are dedicated to death, who are preoccupied with crematoria, *einsatzgruppen,* phenol injections. You would like to declaim on the death of heroes, but for us the noble and brave are those who sanctify life."

As to the second question—on what did it depend whether a man remained a man—the writers appear to have a two-sided reply. There are those, like Frankl and Heimler, who avow that some prisoners preserved their humanity by finding a meaning to account for their suffering. They needed to believe that their imprisonment was a spiritual test, and that if they had the luck and strength to survive, the purpose of what they had endured would one day be revealed to them. Moreover, as they wanted to be "worthy" of their suffering, the more the Nazis tried to degrade them, the more they exercised spiritual resistance.

Conversely, there are those writers who found no meaning in their suffering. Given the organized madness and murder of the Holocaust, they probably would concur with Swift's saying that "meaning is a light rider and easily shook off." Far from ennobling them, their suffering often as not reduced them to the level of animals.

Nonetheless, the one positive value which they commonly recognize as having emerged from their trials is the primacy of human relationships. If there was any "meaning" in hell, it was manifest in the compassion and generosity with which some prisoners responded to their fellow prisoners. Convinced that suffering diminishes a man, they willingly assumed the responsibility to ease the pain of men victimized by oppression and injustice. Thus they might well have adopted for their credo the one voiced in *The Town Beyond the Wall*: "You suffer, therefore I am."

Primo Levi writes in *If This Is a Man* that the "simple and incomprehensible" stories the prisoners exchanged with one another may be seen as the stories of a new Bible. To this metaphor I would add that it is a Bible that both helps define the nature of post-Auschwitz man and measures his values—values in the sense intended by Steven S. Schwarzschild when he writes ("Jewish Values in the Post-Holocaust Future," *Judaism*, Summer 1967):

> What do we know now about man that we did not know before he created Maidenek? By what values shall we try to live that have been seared into our flesh in Bergen-Belsen? What new Jewish actions have been commanded

by the loudspeakers in Buchenwald? . . . In short, what will the story of tomorrow have to look like which we know to be, to be able to be, and to have been what Rousset called *L'universe concentrationnaire?*

Schwarzschild's question, "By what values shall we try to live that have been seared into our flesh in Bergen-Belsen?" is especially pertinent here. How would some of the survivor-writers respond to this query? I can imagine them replying succinctly and in the idiom of the Ten Commandments:

THOU SHALT NOT BE THE EXECUTIONER. Executioner in the sense meant by Primo Levi when he writes in *If This Is a Man*: "Take care not to inflict on each other in your houses what you suffered here." Which is, of course, another way of stating Camus's admonition in *The Plague*: "Each one of us has the plague [that is, Hitler-Eichmann-Himmler impulses] within us. . . . We must keep endless watch on ourselves lest in a careless moment we breathe in somebody's face."

THOU SHALT NOT BE SILENT. This is a view which nearly all of the survivor-writers espouse; namely, that a man does not have the moral right to separate himself from the problems and responsibilities of his community. By extension, then, Wiesel and other survivor-writers would assert that in a time of danger to personal freedom men must have the courage to speak out. Not to do so is to choose, in the Sartrean sense of the word, the role of victim—and, in some instances, the executioner's accomplice.

THOU SHALT NOT BE THE SPECTATOR. As, for example, the spectator in *The Town Beyond the Wall* who was indifferent and unfeeling while witnessing the persecution of his Jewish neighbors. For him the oppressed in the street below his window were as cardboard silhouettes, not flesh and blood. Their suffering impinged on him merely as an abstraction. Hence he was guilty of what Sartre refers to as the "ultimate evil." ("The ultimate evil is to make abstract that which is concrete"

—the "concrete" here being the anguish of pitifully harassed, frightened people.)

THOU SHALT NOT BE THE "DOG." The reference here is to *The Last of the Just* and Ernie Levy's attempt to "leap beyond" his humanity by assuming the guise of a callous, brutish non-Jew in Marseilles. For a brief time, he behaved like the Nazis in that he turned away from what Aldous Huxley has called the "unreasoned tradition of civilized conduct, the conventions of ordinary decency"; therein, Schwarz-Bart reminds us of what can happen to those who become "less than human."

THOU SHALT NOT LOOK TOO LONG INTO THE FIRE. It is important never to forget. Still, to dwell too exclusively and obsessively on the pain and loss of the Holocaust past is to invite the risk of deadening one's capacity to perceive what is life-giving in the present. Hence in *Tell Me Another Morning,* the protagonist, rather than focus on the plentiful objects of death behind the barbed wire in Auschwitz, responds to flowers, sunsets, the sky, birds, the warmth and sustenance of human friendship. So, too, Gregor of *The Gates of the Forest* is drawn to the joyous singing and dancing of some Hasids in a Brooklyn synagogue. Here Wiesel seems to be saying to the reader—We must somehow teach ourselves to live with fervor. Much better that than to carry on as though we were perpetually attached to sackcloth and ashes.

THOU SHALT CONTINUE TO INTERROGATE. As though they were holding up lanterns against a hideous darkness, men posing questions of the Holocaust confer honor upon the deepest reaches of their humanity. Such questioning is akin to the burning of the Eternal Light in the Chamber of Destruction on Mt. Zion or in the memorial Shrine of Yad Vashem on Har Hazikaron. Again, it asks us how we feel about those religious martyrs who went to their deaths in the spirit of the *kiddush ha-shem* tradition. Or how we respond to the charge that many European Jews, in trusting that life would somehow go on as usual during the Nazi occupation, were the paralyzed victims of a "death instinct." Or how we evaluate the opposing views of those who pay homage to the Jewish fighters in the ghettos and forests and those who condemn such physical resistance as undignified and unworthy of Jews.

Finally, and perhaps more importantly, such interrogation asks us how we would have acted had it been our fate to have been trapped in a camp or closed ghetto. And even though we cannot, to be sure, be certain of how we actually would have conducted ourselves under intolerable pressures, nonetheless our concerned involvement in the dialectic of question and response is important. For the writer and reader such interrogation is a way, in Elie Wiesel's words, of taking the Holocaust upon ourselves, of "entering" it.

Notes

1. Quoted by Elie Wiesel, in "Eichmann's Victims and the Unheard Testimony," *Commentary*, December 1961.
2. Elie Wiesel, "Auschwitz—Another Planet," *Hadassah Magazine*, January 1967, p. 15.
3. Elie Wiesel, in "Jewish Values in the Post-Holocaust Future," *Judaism*, Summer 1967, p. 285.
4. Elie Wiesel, "On Being a Jew," *Jewish Heritage*, Summer 1967. Wiesel writes: "The Jew is best characterized by his waiting, by his questioning."
5. Elie Wiesel, "An Appointment with Hate," *Commentary*, December 1962. In this article, Wiesel argues that there is a psychological necessity for Jews to hate certain qualities which "persist" in and "personify" the older generation of postwar Germany.
6. Wiesel has stated, both in print and in public lectures, that world Jewry largely abandoned European Jewry. See, for example, "Jewish Values in the Post-Holocaust Future," *Judaism*, Summer 1967: "Never before have so many Jews been abandoned by so many Jews. The massacre in Europe had almost no bearing on American Jewish life. . . . Tea parties, card games, musical soirees continued to take place. Of course, money was raised, but entertainment was not omitted from the program. In certain free countries of Europe, the situation was not better—perhaps, even worse. When consulted by their governments whether to bring in refugees, some communal leaders had to answer, and their answer was less than enthusiastic." (P. 282.)
7. A frequent descriptive phrase in Wiesel's writing.
8. In Wiesel's eyes all Jews living today—and not only those who came out of the camps and the destroyed Jewish communities of Europe—are survivors in the sense that they are all witnesses. Hence

the perspective for the following statement in an article, "On Being a Jew," *Jewish Heritage,* Summer 1967: "We are all survivors. We are all witnesses. We all embody the intense destiny of our people —a destiny which resists being divided into sections and selected periods. . . . Each of us is therefore responsible for the past and future of Israel, because each of us carries within himself the vision of Sinai and the flames of the *Khourban.*" (Pp. 53–54.)

9. Eugene Heimler, *Concentration Camp,* p. 189.

10. Wiesel, in "Jewish Values in the Post-Holocaust Future," *Judaism,* Summer 1967, p. 288.

11. *Ibid.,* p. 285.

12. Bernd Naumann, *Auschwitz,* p. 132.

13. Wiesel, "Eichmann's Victims and the Unheard Testimony," *Commentary,* December 1961.

14. *Ibid.*

15. George Steiner, "Postscript to a Tragedy," *Encounter,* February 1967.

16. See Dr. Saul Esh, "The Dignity of the Destroyed: Towards a Definition of the Period of the Holocaust," *Judaism,* Vol. II, No. 2 (1962): "What was the general reaction of the Jewish masses, especially in Eastern Europe to the Nazi horror? It was fundamentally what might be called *kiddush ha-hayyim,* the sanctification of life, the overwhelming impulse to preserve life in the midst of death. . . . This expression is taken from one who heard it as the epigram of the late Rabbi Isaac Nissenbaum, one of the known leaders of Polish Jewry, in the years 1940–1941, in the Warsaw Ghetto: 'This is a time for *kiddush ha-hayyim,* the sanctification of life, and not for *kiddush ha-shem,* the holiness of martyrdom. Previously, the Jew's enemy sought his soul and the Jew sacrificed his body in martyrdom [i.e., he made a point of preserving what the enemy wished to take from him]; now the oppressor demands the Jew's body and the Jew is obliged therefore to defend it, to preserve his life.' That *kiddush ha-hayyim* was to all accounts and purposes the general feeling is borne out by all the evidence. It explains the enormous will to live that was emphasized at all times and in all places, in the midst of the basest degradation, a will best expressed by the Yiddish word that was on the lips of the majority of the survivors of the Holocaust—*iberlebyn,* to survive, to remain alive. The Jews of Eastern Europe felt in fact that victory over the enemy lay in their continued existence, for the enemy desired their extinction. . . . ('However wretched existence may be, it is a *mitzvah* to exist.')" (Pp. 166–167.)

17. Frankl's phrase "knowing how to die" evokes the following information in Gideon Hausner's *Justice in Jerusalem:* "A rabbi or

a spiritual leader would often address the community. Some of the speeches were recorded by survivors: 'We are suffering the worst fate of all Jewish generations,' said Rabbi Nachum of Kowel. 'In a few minutes we will fall into this open grave, and nobody will even know where we were buried nor recite a prayer for us. And we so much yearn to live. . . . In this moment let us unite in the supreme wish to sacrifice to the glory of God even our desire to have somebody to pray for us. Let us face the Germans with joy for sanctifying the Lord's name.' Then Joseph Avrech, a teacher, spoke: 'We erected here an edifice of culture and learning that is now being destroyed. My heart breaks when I see this magnificent youth, so full of beauty, wisdom and belief, being brought to slaughter.' Turning now to the Germans he said: 'The Jews are eternal. Our people will see your defeat which is near. What a pity that we here won't be able to see it.' A shot from the pistol of Manthei, the local Police commander, silenced the rest of the speech." (P. 185.)

This incident lends validity to Dr. Saul Esh's statement on pages 109 and 110 of his essay, "The Dignity of the Destroyed: Towards a Definition of the Period of the Holocaust," *Judaism,* Vol. II, No. 2 (1962): "Those who found strength in their hearts to sing in their last hours, 'I believe in the coming of the Messiah,' or to express in the steadfastness of their faith the contempt they felt for their German executioners—they, in no uncertain sense, defeated the Nazis' aim of breaking the Jews in body and spirit and of making them into what the Germans imagined them to be, *Untermenschen.*"

18. A form of torture devised by this despicable camp official.

19. Thus the response of another kind of prisoner in Holland, Anne Frank (*Diary of a Young Girl*), to a blue sky and sunny day: "'As long as this exists,' I thought, 'and I may live to see it, this sunshine, the cloudless skies, while this lasts, I cannot be unhappy.'

"'The best remedy for those who are afraid, lonely, or unhappy is to go outside, somewhere where they can be quite alone with the heavens, nature, and God.'" (Pp. 140–141.)

20. Here Frankl has reference to Rilke's saying—*"Wie viel ist aufzuleiden!"* (How much suffering there is to get through!). Rilke spoke of "getting through suffering" as others would talk of "getting through work."

21. Frankl's remarks about the importance of suffering as an opportunity for spiritual growth are analogous to the views of Hanns Lilje in *The Valley of the Shadow.* Lilje, a member of the German clergy, was imprisoned by the Nazis because of his outspoken criticism of the Third Reich. Recalling a time when increasing nightly Allied air raids turned the existence of prisoners

into a nightmare, Lilje writes: "To be brought face to face with death gives a certain inward nobility to a human being. . . . The person who is threatened by death feels prouder than the man who feels secure, for spiritual freedom is enhanced for those who have ceased to cling to life." (Pp. 75–76.)

22. Cf. the advice a Barrack Elder gave to Alexander Donat (*The Holocaust Kingdom*) when the latter arrived in Maidenek: " 'This is a K.L.,' he said. 'Remember those two initials, K.L. . . . *Konzentrationslager*. You've been brought here to be destroyed by hunger, beating, hard labor, and sickness. You'll be eaten by lice, you'll rot in your own shit.

" 'Let me give you one piece of advice: forget who and what you were. This is a jungle and here the only law is the law of the strongest. No one here is a Mr. Director or a *Herr Doktor*. Everyone here is the same; everyone here is shit.'

"And Donat recalls one of the inmates whose constantly reiterated motto was 'Don't forget, you must die so that I may live.' Again, a Kapo once told Donat: 'I . . . if only one of us is to survive, I want to be that one. No matter what the cost.' " (Pp. 168–169.)

23. See the resolve of Tania in Zdena Berger's novel *Tell Me Another Morning*: "The only thing that remains is the I in me. I find suddenly some strange pleasure in knowing that when I die I will die the same, unchanged, as when I was me. It matters very much. Yes, as I was.

"Keep that last thing. Hang on to it as to the last wall." (P. 78.)

24. Becoming "hard" was a necessary defense, a way of establishing distance from one's sufferings. Often this defense took the form of laughter, a desperate laughter. The point is underscored in Eugen Kogon's *The Theory and Practice of Hell* (London: Martin Secker & Warburg, Ltd., 1950): "Men grew hard and many of them had their sensibilities dulled. It was the same process that takes place in war. A cruel laugh, a brutal jest were often no more than protective devices for minds in danger of becoming hysterical or unhinged. There were many dead martyrs in the camps, but few living saints. . . . We laughed, wretched souls that we were, lest we grow petrified and die." (P. 277.)

Another way in which a prisoner became "hard" was to disassociate himself emotionally, as much as possible, from the horrors around him. Presumably, then, one could, in time, "get used" to the nightmare of the camps. In *Human Behavior in the Concentration Camp*, Dr. Elie Cohen describes how such disassociation affected his own behavior on one occasion, when he witnessed the brutal beating of a prisoner by an SS man: "I felt as if I did not belong, as if the business did not concern me; as if 'I were looking at things through a peephole'; I felt untouched by any compassion either for the prisoner, who had probably been beaten to death, or for the incoming labor group." (P. 116.)

So, too, one reads in Kitty Hart's *I Am Alive* how she and other Auschwitz prisoners of a work unit, whose task it was to sort out the clothing of the dead, attempted to disassociate themselves from the horrors around them. She and the others lived in a hut near the crematoria. On occasion they read books, sunbathed, played musical instruments, joked, sang—all this to deaden themselves to what was happening but a few yards away from them: "All around us were screams, death, smoking chimneys making the air black and heavy with soot and the smell of burning bodies. Passing us were women, poor and rich, tired looking, clutching their children and babies. Sometimes a small child wheeled a doll in a little pram, or jumped over a skipping rope. A mother would change a baby while waiting or put a bonnet over a child's head lest the sun would be too hot for it. A child would pick up a flower which grew near the road . . . . All the time we just lay on the lawn and watched." (Pp. 92–93.)

25. Extreme hunger could usurp all feelings of pity and mercy. Starving prisoners stole bread from each other, from the sick and dying and defenseless. While in the sick bay at Amersfoort, Dr. Elie Cohen (*op. cit.,* p. 138) confessed that he "helped the sick to eat, and while grudging them every bite, I would wait until they refused further food and offered me the remainder in gratitude for my 'help.'"

26. Eliezer's attempt here to stay inconspicuous evokes the following statement, which appears in *I Cannot Forgive,* by Rudolph Vrba and Alan Bestic: "Those who were different died in Auschwitz, while the anonymous, the faceless ones, survived" (p. 145).

27. Thus, for example, Leon Wells (*The Janowska Road*) recalls the behavior of prisoners who were waiting to be shot and flung into vast funeral pyres: "I should like to emphasize again that usually the people undress themselves quickly and go to the fire without protest. Some of them even jump into the fire without an order to do so. They have had enough. The tortures have been going on too long. Most of them have already lost all their dear ones, and everyone feels that the world is his enemy; even the children in diapers feel this." (P. 207.)

28. Similarly, Primo Levi concludes his second book, *The Reawakening,* with the description of a recurring dream that disturbs him: "I am alone in the centre of a grey and turbid nothing, and now, I *know* what this thing means, and I also know that I

have always known it: I am in the Lager once more, and nothing is true outside the Lager" (pp. 221–222).

So, too, Olga Lengyel (*Five Chimneys: The Story of Auschwitz*), who as a medical aid in the Auschwitz infirmary took part in the killing of newborn babies to save their mothers from the gas chambers, cries out: "And so the Germans succeeded in making murderers of even us. To this day the picture of these murdered babies haunts me." (Pp. 100–101.)

29. See Anatoly Kuznetsov's essay "The Memories" in *The New York Times Book Review*, April 9, 1967.

30. Frankl's utterance here evokes the words of the unnamed singer in Psalm 116: "For thou hast delivered my soul from death, mine eyes from tears, and my feet from falling. I will walk before the LORD in the land of the living."

31. Cf. the friendship in the camps described by Earl Weinstock and Herbert Wilner in *The Seven Years*, pp. 92–94. In a Transnistria camp, an older man, Micklos, befriends the boy Weinstock and teaches him "to think clearly." Weinstock recalls that "for me there was Micklos, and he filled my mind with his kind of learning, and he filled it with hope."

32. Like Heimler, Primo Levi was determined to survive so that he could "bear witness," as note the following passage in *If This Is a Man:* "Even in this place one can survive, and therefore one must want to survive, to tell the story, to bear witness. . . . We are slaves, condemned of every right, exposed to every insult, condemned to certain death, but we still possess one power, and we must defend it with all our strength for it is the last—the power to refuse our consent. So we must certainly wash our faces without soap in dirty water and dry ourselves on our jackets. We must polish our shoes, not because the regulation states it, but for dignity and propriety. We must walk erect, without dragging our feet, not in homage to Prussian discipline but to remain alive, not to begin to die." (P. 36.)

33. Emmanuel Ringelblum, social historian, teacher, scholar and archivist of the Warsaw ghetto, was founder of the Oneg Shabbat (Sabbath celebrants), the secret archives of the ghetto. Ringelblum and his fellow archivists collected some 103 volumes of memoirs, German official documents, and various reports on the resistance movement in Poland. He also wrote accounts of the underground movement which were smuggled out of the ghetto and dispatched to Jewish communities around the world, so that they might be alerted to the tragedy of Polish Jewry. His journals cover day-to-day events in the ghetto from January 1940 to early 1943. Although he had a rare opportunity to be rescued by the Polish

underground, Ringelblum refused to leave Warsaw because of his commitment as the chief archivist in the ghetto. He believed that in continuing to serve in this role he was fulfilling his obligations to his people; and he hoped that his journals and the records of the Oneg Shabbat would be preserved as a legacy for posterity. The Nazis murdered him and his family in 1944. He was then forty-four years old. After the war, Ringelblum's notes were found in rubber-sealed milk cans under the ruins of the Warsaw ghetto.

34. Especially important are the chronicles of Bernard Goldstein, Herman Kruk, Zelig Kalmanovitch, and Mary Berg.

Goldstein is an author of *Five Years in the Warsaw Ghetto* (originally published as *The Stars Bear Witness*) (Dolphin Books, Doubleday & Company, Inc., 1961). A leader of the Socialist Labor Union—the Bund—Goldstein was widely admired and respected by Jewish workers for his various abilities, principled conduct, and immense courage. When Hitler began marching eastward, Goldstein took an active part in defending the Jewish populace against attacks by Polish anti-Semitic hooligans. After the Nazis occupied Warsaw, he joined the Jewish underground. He was fated to survive the destruction of the ghetto. His book records events in the ghetto of Warsaw from October 1939 to June 1945.

Herman Kruk came to Vilna from Warsaw, where he had been the director of the Grosser Library. His *Diary of the Vilna Ghetto* mirrors the plight of Vilna Jewry from June 1941 to mid-1943. Shortly thereafter he was taken by the Germans to an extermination center in Estonia, where he died at the age of forty-seven. After the liberation of Vilna, a typescript of the diary was found in one of the bunkers built by ghetto fighters. In 1961 the diary was published by the YIVO Institute for Jewish Research in New York.

Zelig Kalmanovitch was an erudite scholar in Yiddish philology and Semitic history, and one of the founders of the Yiddish Scientific Institute in Vilna. The first entry in his "A Diary of the Nazi Ghetto in Vilna" (*YIVO Annual of Jewish Social Science,* Vol. VIII), begins on June 22, 1941, and thereafter registers in Hebrew his day-to-day impressions of ghetto life under Nazi occupation until June 1943. In September 1943 he and his wife were deported to Estonia, where they perished. The diary was found by Herman Kruk and cached in the ghetto library, where it was discovered intact after the liberation of Vilna.

When she was imprisoned in the Warsaw ghetto and began writing in her diary, Mary Berg was sixteen years old. Finally permitted (due to her status as the daughter of an American citizen) to leave Warsaw, she smuggled out her diary. Shortly after her arrival in the United States in 1944, she rewrote the diary and it was published the following year. It is one of the first extended accounts of the establishment and destruction of the Warsaw ghetto.

35. Writer, Hebrew scholar, and educator, Kaplan served as the principal of a Warsaw elementary Hebrew day school for some forty years. During the Nazi occupation Kaplan kept an almost daily record of events from the outbreak of war to the time of his deportation; the diary was written in Hebrew. His wife and he perished at Treblinka. Some twenty years after the Warsaw ghetto was destroyed, Kaplan's diaries were discovered by Abraham I. Katsh of New York University, and in 1965 they were published by The Macmillan Company under the title *Scroll of Agony*.

Why the title? There is a possible clue in his diaries. Kaplan relates that some rabbis from Praga, who had been forced by the Nazis to leave their homes there, appeared in Warsaw, carrying their scroll of the Torah, which Kaplan refers to as "scroll of agony": "The scroll of agony which the rabbis of Praga unrolled before us touched our souls. Even the stouthearted ones in the audience could not hold back their tears. One rabbi related, 'Today a Jew ran into my home who had been driven almost mad. He was holding a scroll of the Torah: "My family and I are rolling in the dungheaps; in my home there was this scroll of the Torah. Please, rabbi, take this, my most sacred possession, and guard it as the apple of your eye. Nothing is left to us but this Torah."'" (P. 217.) So there was a connection in Kaplan's mind between the scrolls of such Torahs and the scroll of agony, his diary, which he was determined to preserve, just as the rabbis of Praga wanted to safeguard their scrolls.

36. See the plaint of a child separated from her father in a brief poem, "I Sit with My Eyes," written by an anonymous little girl during the Holocaust.

> "I sit with my dolls by the stove and dream.
> I dream that my father came back,
> I dream that my father is still alive.
> How good it is to have a father.
> I do not know where my father is."
> (Translated from the Yiddish by Joseph Leftwich)

The terror and desperation of Jewish children in the ghetto is nowhere more disquietingly marked than in the following sentences from the May 9, 1940 entry in the journal of Emmanuel Ringelblum (*Notes from the Warsaw Ghetto*): "—In a refugee center an eight-year-old child went mad. Screamed, 'I want to steal, I want to rob, I want to eat, I want to be a German.' In his hunger he hated being Jewish."

37. Kaplan's outcry here is not far from the tenor of Job's lament: "From out of the city the dying groan, and the soul of the wounded cries for help; yet God pays no attention to their prayer." Cf. also the Jobian question in Alexander Donat, *The Holocaust Kingdom:* "Above all we [Warsaw Jewry] kept asking ourselves the age-old question: *why, why?* What was all that suffering for? What had we done to deserve this hurricane of evil, this avalanche of cruelty?" (P. 100.)

Less than a year after this entry, Kaplan was still asking the same question. "Has Israel no God? Why has He refrained from giving us aid in our time of trouble?" (P. 209.) Similarly, on June 27, 1942, he wrote: "God of Gods! Shall the sword devour thy sons forever?"

38. Cf. *Notes from the Warsaw Ghetto: The Journal of Emmanuel Ringelblum:* "If the war is to last as long as the Jews can hold out, that would be bad because the Jews can hold out longer than the war can last." (Pp. 42–43.) And Ringelblum notes elsewhere (p. 66) that a woman in the ghetto, in answer to a German official who told her, "See to it that you disappear!" replied, "I am not air to disappear!"

39. Another act of incomprehensible cruelty is described in Hausner's *Justice in Jerusalem,* the account of one of the witnesses for the prosecution at the Eichmann trial, Noah Zabludowicz: "Once I saw an SS officer in Ciechanów politely asking a Jewish mother in the street to let him try to appease her crying baby. With incredulity in her eyes and with trembling hands the woman delivered the infant, whereupon the Nazi smashed the baby's small head on the sharp edge of the curbstone. The mother did not even have time to cry out. At that moment I thought God had hidden his face from the human race." (P. 163.)

40. Concerning the Nazis' common reference to Jews as vermin, see, for example, the "pep talk" by Himmler to a squad of *Einsatzkomandos* (soldiers who were assigned to mass murder Jews and other "enemies of the Third Reich") in *Justice in Jerusalem:* " 'Look at nature,' he said. 'Creatures that are too tired to fight go under.' He repeated Hitler's favorite parallel between biological phenomena and moral actions. 'A bug or a rat has a right to live, as a thistle has a right to grow. Yet men exterminate vermin and weed out thistles. This is in self-defense, otherwise vermin will kill men and thistles will destroy the crop.' " (P. 88.) And on another occasion, Himmler said: "Anti-Semitism is exactly the same as

delousing. Getting rid of lice is not a question of ideology; it is a matter of cleanliness."

41. This same spirit of dedication is evident in Kaplan's entry of August 27, 1940: "There is no end to our scroll of agony. I am afraid that the impressions of this terrible era will be lost because they have not been adequately recorded. I risk my life with my writing, but my abilities are limited; I don't know all the facts; those that I do know may not be sufficiently clear; and many of them I write on the basis of rumors whose accuracy I cannot guarantee. But for the sake of truth, I do not require individual facts, but rather the manifestations which are the fruits of a great many facts that leave their impression on the people's opinions, on their mood and morale. And I can guarantee the factualness of these manifestations because I dwell among my people and behold their misery and their souls' torments." (*Scroll of Agony*, p. 189.)

42. See Jacob Robinson, *And the Crooked Shall Be Made Straight*, p. 223.

43. Such committees were elected by the residents of a group of tenement buildings facing a common courtyard.

44. See Kaplan's description of these groups: "Every courtyard committee is divided into reporting subcommittees (financial, sanitary, educational affairs, political affairs, apartments, dress, food supplies, etc.), and each of these is further divided and subdivided, and in this way everyone is kept busy." (*Scroll of Agony*, p. 228.)

45. See Kaplan's reference to these gardens: "Nursery schools bring their infant charges to the gardens, and older children have their lessons there. In short: an arrow in the Nazis' eyes! The arteries of life do not stop pulsing. We are schooled in life, skilled in the art of living; it is like the words of the prophet: 'When thou walkest through the fire thou shalt not be burned; neither shall the flame kindle upon thee!' " (*Scroll of Agony*, p. 294.)

46. The German Command also forbade dancing but this did not prevent the populace from holding dances. And Kaplan refers to the latter as still another expression of the community's spiritual resistance against the enemy: "There is a lot of frivolity in the ghetto, in order to somewhat lessen its sorrow. In the daytime, when the sun is shining, the ghetto groans. But at night everyone is dancing even though his stomach is empty. Quiet, discreet evening music accompanies the dancing. It is almost a *mitzvah* to dance. The more one dances, the more it is a sign of his belief in the 'eternity of Israel.' Every dance is a protest against our oppressors." (*Scroll of Agony*, pp. 244–245.)

47. Cf. a similar point of view expressed by Marie Syrkin in "The Literature of the Holocaust," *Midstream*, May 1966: "We

hesitate to apply the usual canons to the immense mass of written material about the destruction of the Jews already available and still being produced in various languages. Our qualms inhibit judgment, yet we continue to read not only because we are in search of some supreme artistic expression but because we are still grappling intellectually and morally with what happened."

48. The realm of the inhuman—that state of mind wherein men are disposed to seeing only the stranger and not the brother in other men—is an important theme in Holocaust literature. This theme is present, for example, in Primo Levi's *If This Is a Man* when some morally callous civilians turn up their noses in disgust on seeing starving, emaciated, unbathed prisoners in Auschwitz. Again, the realm of the inhuman is evidenced in Hochhuth's *The Deputy* when the Cardinal replies to the suggestion of the heroic priest, Riccardo, that the Pope speak out against the Nazi persecution of European Jewry: "The Chief, mmm, what, is risking a great deal if he intervenes for the Jews. Minorities are never popular in any country and the Jews have been provoking the Germans for years, have they not? . . . Pogroms just don't happen."

49. Of such survivors, who dangle between the realms of the living and the dead, Nelly Sachs has written:

> "We beg of you:
> Do not show us a barking dog as yet.
> It could be, it just could be
> That we shall disintegrate into dust,
> Turn into dust before your eyes.
> For what keeps our substance together?"

50. In Wiesel's account ("The Last Return," *Commentary*, March 1965) of his revisit to his hometown in Transylvania, the following passage testifies to the thoroughness of the Jewish community's destruction: "I searched for the people out of my past, I searched for my past, and I did not find them. Why was everything so calm in front of the Talmud-Torah Synagogue and the Wishnitzer *shtibel?* I looked for Kalman the Kabbalist, Moshe the Madman, Shmukler the Prince, Leizer the Fat: vanished without a trace as though carried off by one of the 'antipersonnel' neutron bombs that destroys people and spares the stones they call their property."

51. See Wiesel's reminiscence, "My Teachers," in *Jewish Heritage*, Fall 1966, for an admission of the important influence that various teachers of his youth had on him.

52. Similarly, in *The Holocaust Kingdom*, Alexander Donat la-

ments that after the liberation of Maidenek by General Patton's Third Army, the prisoners were unable to "square debts" with their former oppressors: "We had the souls of pogroms and ghettos, two thousand years of the Sixth Commandment had tamed and blunted in us the natural virile impulse of revenge. The sublime words, 'Thou shalt not kill,' which had been our shield against murder and persecution became the shield and protector of a nation of murderers and our alibi for our cowardice and weakness." (Pp. 290–291.)

53. "My entire work is based on the difficulty of killing, or of committing suicide," Elie Wiesel said in 1963 in an interview with a reporter from *L'Express.*

54. Cf. the following statement by Wiesel in "Jewish Values in the Post-Holocaust Future," a symposium in *Judaism,* Summer 1967: "I do not like to think of the Jew as suffering. I prefer thinking of him as someone who can defeat suffering—his own and others. For his is a Messianic dimension; he can save the world from a new Auschwitz. As Camus would say: one must create happiness to protest against a universe of unhappiness. But— one *must* create it. And we are creating it. We were creating it. Jews got married, celebrated weddings, had children within the ghetto walls. Their absurd faith in their non-existent future was, nevertheless, *af al pi chen,* an affirmation of the spirit." (P. 291.)

55. One is reminded of the famous historian Simon Dubnow's statement: "Jewry, being a spiritual unity, cannot suffer annihilation. The body, the mold, may be destroyed; the spirit is immortal."

56. The Rabbi's assertion is not dissimilar in tone and content to the following comment made by Wiesel during the *Judaism* symposium of "Jewish Values in the Post-Holocaust Future": "The Jew, in my view, may rise against God, provided he remains within God. One can be a very good Jew, observe all the mitzvot, study Talmud—and yet be against God. *Af al pi chen velamrot hakol*—as if to say: You, God, do not want me to be Jewish; well, Jewish we shall be nevertheless, despite Your will."

57. Jakov Lind's *Soul of Wood* relates the surrealistic-like relationship of Wohlbrecht, a crippled World War I veteran who has a wooden leg, and a young Jew, Anton Barth, who has a totally paralyzed body.

58. Lind's "cool" in writing on the Holocaust is nowhere better evidenced than in a paragraph in *Landscape in Concrete* where the narrator describes the murders: "With his left hand Bachmann held the back of Thor's neck and with his right cut him open from throat to abdomen. He had to step aside quickly, for the blood gushed like a spring when the stone is taken away. A man is full

of blood, the way a balloon is full of air. It was always fun to burst balloons, it made a bang, it was exciting. A man doesn't make any bang. Thor wheezed and collapsed. The knife had gone through part of the windpipe. Bachmann let him down slowly with his left hand. Wouldn't want the poor kid to fall on his head." (P. 100.)

59. Borowski, a Polish non-Jew, was a prisoner in Dachau and Auschwitz from 1943 to 1945. He survived this ordeal but in 1951 committed suicide in Warsaw.

60. One must talk of miracles in referring to the creative spirit that was abundantly present in this ghetto. As early as 1942, lectures, readings, operas, concerts, and dramatic productions were performed in the ghetto. We know, for example, that Smetna's *Bartered Bride* and works of Mozart and Bizet were presented, that the opera *Brundibar* was presented by children and performances of Schiller's *Marie Stuart* and a fairy tale by Capek were staged.

61. Educator, physician, and writer, Dr. Janusz Korczak was director of the largest Jewish orphanage in Warsaw. He was sixty-four when the Nazis murdered him. At the age of thirty he had given up a successful practice as a doctor in order to teach orphans. On August 6, 1942, he and some two hundred children of the orphanage were ordered by the SS to be taken off for "resettlement." So he placed himself at the head of the children, and they went through the streets toward the transport place singing, "We are all brothers"—followed by German guards. It is known that the Judenrat offered him an opportunity to avoid deportation, but he rejected their offer. "I would not leave my children," he was reported to have replied before being loaded into a cattle van with the children and sent off to Treblinka. They were never seen again. But something he once wrote will not easily be forgotten: "There is no end to the desire for goodness. Out of this desire will come the fruit."

62. Rabbi David Shapiro was one of the three rabbis left in the Warsaw ghetto during its final days. All three were offered an opportunity by officials of the Court of the Bishops in Warsaw to escape to safe hiding places in another part of the city. They were asked to deliberate on this unusual offer and make their decision at once.

The three rabbis withdrew to discuss the matter but instead fell into a deep silence. Each wanted to live for himself and for the sake of his family—Rabbi Shapiro had a wife and four children —and yet be true to his moral responsibility as a spiritual leader for the remaining Jews in the ghetto.

Finally, Rabbi Shapiro, the youngest of the three, broke the silence, and he said, as is reported by K. Shabbetai in "As Sheep to the Slaughter" (*World Jewry,* March/April 1963): "I am the youngest present. My words do not bind you. We all of us know perfectly well that we cannot help these folk in any way whatsoever. Yet by the very fact that we stay with them, that we do not forsake them, there is a kind of encouragement, something maybe of the only possible encouragement. I do not have the strength to abandon these people." He had spoken for the others; they were resolved to share the tragic fate of their people. And so their only reply to the offer was, "There cannot be any negotiations about this matter."

Miraculously, Rabbi Shapiro (not so his wife and children) survived the destruction of the ghetto. Today he is the religious leader of the remaining Jewish community in Fuerth, West Germany.

63. "The heaviest burden that men can lay on us is, not that they persecute us with hatred and scorn, but that they thus plant hatred in our souls." The foregoing comment by Spinoza is certainly applicable to Ernie's violent hatred for the Hitler Youth thugs who attacked him.

64. Ernie's choice is identical, in essence, to one made by Hynek Tausig, the main character of "The Return," in Arnost Lustig's collection of short stories entitled *Night and Hope.* For Tausig, like Levy, having escaped from the Nazis, could have enjoyed extended immunity from them; and yet he chose to return to Theresienstadt ghetto, which was a clearance center for the extermination camps.

65. So, too, Jacob Henriques of *Breaking-Point,* in acting (and knowing full well the consequences of such action) to protect the pious Jew, Hirsch, from the brutality of deportation officials, chooses to share the tragic fate of the Jewish people. Previously, Henriques had been bent on saving only his own skin. For interceding in behalf of Hirsch, Henriques is arrested and marked for deportation to an extermination camp.

66. Ernie's relationship to the doomed children also recalls Ilse Aichinger's *Herod's Children,* a classic in postwar German literature. In this novel, the fantasies and daydreams of some Jewish children living in Vienna during the Nazi Occupation and who long for a refuge in America or Palestine, are sensitively rendered. While awaiting deportation to Poland, the children escape from the hard reality of their lives into a make-believe world of happy places and people. For example, at one point in the story, the children express their longing for a journey to Palestine (p. 52).

Bibliography

BOOKS

Aichinger, Ilse, *Herod's Children*. Atheneum Publishers, 1963.
——— *The Origins of Totalitarianism*. Meridian Books, The World Publishing Company, 1958.
Arendt, Hannah, *Eichmann in Jerusalem: A Report on the "Banality of Evil."* The Viking Press, Inc., 1963.
Berg, Mary, *Warsaw Ghetto*, tr. by Norbert Guterman. L. B. Fisher, 1945.
Berger, Zdena, *Tell Me Another Morning*. Harper & Brothers, 1961.
Bettelheim, Bruno, *The Informed Heart*. The Free Press of Glencoe, 1960.
Bor, Josef, *The Terezin Requiem*. Alfred A. Knopf, Inc., 1963.
Camus, Albert, *The Plague*. Alfred A. Knopf, Inc., 1948.
Cohen, Elie, *Human Behavior in the Concentration Camp*. Grosset & Dunlap, Inc., 1953.
Donat, Alexander, *The Holocaust Kingdom*. Holt, Rinehart and Winston, Inc., 1965.
Frank, Anne, *Diary of a Young Girl*. Pocket Books, Inc., 1965.
Frankl, Viktor, *Man's Search for Meaning* (original title: *From Death-Camp to Existentialism*, Beacon Press, Inc., 1959). Beacon Press, Inc., 1963.
Friedlander, Albert H. (ed.), *Out of the Whirlwind: A Reader of the Holocaust Literature*. Union of American Hebrew Congregations, 1968.
Friedman, Philip, *Martyrs and Fighters*. Frederick A. Praeger, Inc., Publisher, 1954.
Glatstein, Jacob, *Gedenklider* ("Memorial Poems"). New York, 1943.
Goldstein, Bernard, *The Stars Bear Witness*. Dolphin Books, Doubleday & Company, Inc., 1949.
Habe, Hans, *The Mission*. Coward-McCann, Inc., 1966.
Hart, Kitty, *I Am Alive*. London: Abelard-Schuman, Ltd., 1961.

Hausner, Gideon, *Justice in Jerusalem.* Harper & Row, Publishers, Inc., 1966.
Heimler, Eugene, *Concentration Camp* (original title: *Night of the Mist,* The Vanguard Press, Inc., 1959). Pyramid Books, 1961.
Hersey, John, *The Wall.* Alfred A. Knopf, Inc., 1950.
Hilberg, Raul, *The Destruction of the European Jews.* Quadrangle Books, Inc., 1961.
Hochhuth, Rolf, *The Deputy.* Grove Press, Inc., 1964.
Kaplan, Chaim, *Scroll of Agony: The Warsaw Diary of Chaim A. Kaplan,* tr. and ed. by Abraham I. Katsh. The Macmillan Company, 1965.
Ka-tzetnik, *Atrocity.* Lyle Stuart, Publisher, 1963.
——— *House of Dolls.* Pyramid Books, 1960.
Kogon, Eugen, *The Theory and Practice of Hell.* London: Martin Secker & Warburg, Ltd., 1950.
Kosinski, Jerzy, *The Painted Bird.* Houghton Mifflin Company, 1965.
Kruk, Herman, *Diary of the Vilna Ghetto.* YIVO Institute for Jewish Research, 1961.
Langfus, Anna, *The Whole Land Brimstone.* Pantheon Books, Inc., 1962.
Lengyel, Olga, *Five Chimneys: The Story of Auschwitz.* Ziff-Davis Publishing Company, 1947.
Levi, Primo, *If This Is a Man,* tr. by Stuart Woolf. Orion Press, Inc., 1959. (Published as *Survival in Auschwitz* by Collier Books, 1961.)
——— *The Reawakening.* Little, Brown and Company, 1965.
Levin, Meyer, *The Stronghold.* Simon and Schuster, Inc., 1963.
Levin, Nora, *The Holocaust: The Destruction of European Jewry, 1933–1945.* Thomas Y. Crowell Company, 1968.
Lilje, Hanns, *The Valley of the Shadow.* Muhlenberg Press, 1950.
Lind, Jakov, *Landscape in Concrete,* tr. by Ralph Manheim. Grove Press, Inc., 1966.
——— *Soul of Wood.* London: Jonathan Cape, Ltd., 1964.
Maurel, Michelene, *An Ordinary Camp.* Simon and Schuster, Inc., 1958.
Memmi, Albert, *Portrait of a Jew.* Orion Press, Inc., 1962.
Morse, Arthur D., *While Six Million Died: A Chronicle of American Apathy.* Random House, Inc., 1968.
Naumann, Bernd, *Auschwitz.* Frederick A. Praeger, Inc., 1966.
Nyiszli, Miklos, *Auschwitz: A Doctor's Eye-Witness Account.* Frederick Fell, Inc., 1960.

Pawlowicz, Sala, *I Will Survive*. W. W. Norton & Company, Inc., 1962.

Poliakov, Leon, *Harvest of Hate: The Nazi Program for the Destruction of Jews of Europe*. London: Elek Books, Ltd., 1956.

Presser, Jacob, *Breaking-Point*. Popular Library, Inc., 1959.

Rawicz, Piotr, *Blood from the Sky*. Harcourt, Brace and World, Inc., 1964.

Reitlinger, Gerald, *The Final Solution: The Attempt to Exterminate the Jews of Europe, 1939–1945*. Beechhurst, Inc., 1953.

Ringelblum, Emmanuel, *Notes from the Warsaw Ghetto: The Journal of Emmanuel Ringelblum*. McGraw-Hill Book Company, Inc., 1958.

Robinson, Jacob, *And the Crooked Shall Be Made Straight*. The Macmillan Company, 1965.

Sachs, Nelly, *O the Chimneys*. Farrar, Straus and Giroux, Inc., 1967.

Schwarz-Bart, André, *The Last of the Just*. Bantam Books, Inc., 1961.

Semprun, Jorge, *The Long Voyage*. Grove Press, Inc., 1964.

Tennenbaum, Joseph, *Underground: The Story of a People*. Philosophical Library, 1951.

Vrba, Rudolph, and Bestic, Alan, *I Cannot Forgive*. Grove Press, Inc., 1964.

Weinstock, Earl, and Wilner, Herbert, *The Seven Years*. E. P. Dutton & Company, Inc., 1959.

Wells, Leon, *The Janowska Road*. The Macmillan Company, 1963.

Wiesel, Elie, *The Accident*. Hill & Wang, Inc., 1961.

——— *A Beggar in Jerusalem*. Random House, Inc., 1970.

——— *Dawn*. Hill & Wang, Inc., 1962.

——— *The Gates of the Forest*. Holt, Rinehart and Winston, Inc., 1966.

——— *Night*. Hill & Wang, Inc., 1961.

——— *The Town Beyond the Wall*. Atheneum Publishers, 1964.

PERIODICALS

Alvarez, A., "The Literature of the Holocaust," *Commentary*, November 1964.

Bialer, Tosia, "Behind the Wall," *Collier's*, February 20 and 27, 1943.

Borowski, T., "This Way for the Gas," *Commentary,* July 1962.
———— "The People Who Walked," *Commentary,* February
    1967.
Capouya, Emile, "The Cry of the Forsaken," *Saturday Review,*
    May 28, 1966.
Daiches, David, "After Such Knowledge . . ." *Commentary,*
    December 1965.
Esh, Saul, "The Dignity of the Destroyed: Towards a Definition
    of the Period of the Holocaust," *Judaism,* Vol. II, No. 2
    (1962).
Frankel, Theodore, "Out of Auschwitz—Balm?" *Midstream,*
    December 1964.
Friedman, Joseph, "The Shame of Survival," *Saturday Review,*
    July 25, 1964.
Kalmanovitch, Zelig, "A Diary of the Nazi Ghetto in Vilna,"
    YIVO Annual of Jewish Social Science, Vol. VIII (1953).
Kuznetsov, Anatoly, "The Memories," *The New York Times
    Book Review,* April 9, 1967.
Schwarzschild, Steven, in "Jewish Values in the Post-Holocaust
    Future," *Judaism,* Summer 1967.
Shabbetai, K., "As Sheep to the Slaughter," *World Jewry,*
    March/April 1963.
Steiner, George, "Postscript to a Tragedy," *Encounter,* Febru-
    ary 1967.
———— in "Jewish Values in the Post-Holocaust Future,"
    Judaism, Summer 1967.
Syrkin, Marie, "The Literature of the Holocaust," *Midstream,*
    May 1966.
Wiesel, Elie, "An Appointment with Hate," *Commentary,* De-
    cember 1962.
————"Auschwitz—Another Planet" (a review of Naumann's
    Auschwitz), *Hadassah Magazine,* January 1967.
———— "Eichmann's Victims and the Unheard Testimony,"
    Commentary, December 1961.
———— in "Jewish Values in the Post-Holocaust Future,"
    Judaism, Summer 1967.
———— "The Last Return," *Commentary,* March 1965.
———— "My Teachers," *Jewish Heritage,* Fall 1966.
———— "On Being a Jew," *Jewish Heritage,* Summer 1967.

COLLECTION

Lustig, Arnost, "The Return," *Night and Hope.* London: Hutch-
    inson & Co. (Publishers), Ltd., 1962.